Clau

Salisbury SPCK

C000006050

# Jesus and the Doctrine of the Atonement

# Jesus and the Doctrine of the Atonement

*Biblical notes on a controversial topic*

C. J. den Heyer

SCM PRESS LTD

Translated by John Bowden from the Dutch
*Verzoening. Bijbelse notities bij een omstreden thema,*
published 1997 by Uitgeverij Kok – Kampen.

© Uitgeverij Kok – Kampen 1997

Translation © John Bowden 1998

All rights reserved. No part of this publication
may be reproduced, stored in a retrieval system, or
transmitted, in any form or by any means, electronic,
mechanical, photocopying or otherwise, without the
prior permission of the publisher, SCM Press Ltd.

0 334 02733 0

First published 1998 by
SCM Press Ltd
9–17 St Albans Place London N1 0NX

Typeset by Regent Typesetting, London

Printed in Great Britain by
Biddles Ltd, Guildford and King's Lynn

# Contents

# Preface

Just under two years ago I wrote a book about research into
Jesus over the last 150 years. It was called *Jesus Matters*, and
was an attempt at a stocktaking. The investigation began in the
second half of the eighteenth century, since when countless New
Testament scholars have been involved in it. Other theologians
followed, and interest spread beyond theological circles. That is
still the case today. The distant past makes people curious and
raises questions which are difficult to answer.

Can we really get back to the historical Jesus? Experts do not
agree on a single aspect of the investigation. Opinions are
strongly divided, but almost no one would say that we can discover Jesus as he really was. However, that does not mean that
it is unimportant for theology to get back into the past. By carefully weighing up the facts, making use of well-tried scholarly
methods of historical research, historians can sketch a picture of
Jesus of Nazareth. His career can be reconstructed. Because our
knowledge of the early Jewish world at the beginning of the
Christian era has increased considerably, it is more possible
than it used to be to trace the background to Jesus' words
and investigate them against it. For that reason, at the end of
*Jesus Matters* I ventured to remark that there was a degree of
consensus among New Testament scholars. Although I am convinced that the Gospels cannot be read as biographies of Jesus,
I nevertheless sketched out a 'mini-biography' of Jeshua of
Nazareth as the result of 150 years of research. Jesus was a
human being among other human beings, but also a special
person, inspired and creative, in search of people in need, a man

after God's heart who provoked opposition and ultimately died a violent death on the cross.

I went on to make a discovery. It is not a new one, but I have become more strongly aware of its consequences than ever before. Theology and the church cannot avoid constantly seeking the historical Jesus. Anyone who talks about Jesus Christ must realize that he truly lived: he was the Jew Jeshua of Nazareth, born and brought up in the land of Israel at the beginning of our era. However 'high' the terms used in christology, i.e. the doctrine of the person of Christ, it should never be forgotten that 'the Word became flesh and dwelt among us' (John 1.14).

The question we need to consider here is a complex one. The conclusion which I have just stated seems to conflict with our experience that the historical investigation which is thought to be necessary at the same time creates a gulf between the historical Jesus and the traditional image of Christ as presented in the classical christological dogmas, a gulf which is difficult to bridge. The historian speaks of the human being Jesus of Nazareth. In theology and the church he is called the Son of God. His humiliating death on the cross can be explained historically in every respect: it was the result of a monstrous alliance between Jewish leaders and the Roman forces of occupation, both of whom were interested in making sure that law and order were disturbed as little as possible at the feast of Passover. The cruel death of Jesus was not unique. In the Roman empire it was customary to punish runaway slaves and rebels in this way. The cross has assumed a central place in the course of church history. It functions as the symbol of Jesus' death, which has brought about reconciliation between God and human beings.

The gulf is deep and seems impossible to bridge. The ways of historical research and dogma diverge widely. As I have remarked, I have gradually become increasingly aware of this. Those who engage in an intensive investigation of the historical Jesus find it increasingly difficult to accept christological dogma.

Moreover this book originates in perplexity. I have not written in it in the hope that I shall be able to bridge the gulf indicated above. Those who think that they can bridge this gulf have not realized how far the ways have indeed diverged. Rather, what I have attempted to do is to make a contribution to the necessary process of reflecting on the significance of the life and death of Jesus of Nazareth. Here I shall be doing precisely what the early Christian community also did: looking for words, images and metaphors which express this significance. We live almost two thousand years later. We have to look for new words, images and metaphors. However, in our quest we can gratefully make use of what is offered us in the New Testament and the Christian tradition.

At the end of this preface I owe readers an explanation of my way of working. This book has no 'notes'. There were notes in the drafts which preceded the final text. But after careful consideration I decided to scrap them all. There is so much literature about reconciliation and the doctrine of the atonement that if I were to refer to it all, readers would lose sight of the 'scriptural' wood in all the theological trees which have grow up. When I realized that, I began all over again. I put all the scholarly literature back into my bookcase – and readers must take my word that my study had books and articles on this topic strewn all over it. Then I wrote the chapters which now follow with no more than the Bible in the original languages, some translations, a dictionary and a concordance. Sometimes I consulted a commentary. I also relied on my memory and the knowledge that I have acquired over thirty years of theological work. So in all modesty, here I offer my findings to interested readers, in the hope that they may make a useful contribution to a process of reflection.

# The Crucified Jesus

*In the fifteenth year of the emperor Tiberius*

Jesus grew up in Nazareth, a small town in Galilee. We know little for certain about his youth. He was the oldest child in the family of Joseph and Mary. The inhabitants of Nazareth knew him as the carpenter (Mark 6.3). As an adult, at a particular moment Jesus underwent a far-reaching change. He left his home in Nazareth and began to travel around Galilee. He attracted attention and gathered a group of disciples around him. All four canonical Gospels presuppose a direct connection between this change in Jesus' life and the appearance of John the Baptist (Mark 1.11; Matt. 3.1–17; Luke 3.21–22; John 1.19–34).

According to the evangelist Luke, this event took place 'in the fifteenth year of the reign of the emperor Tiberius' (Luke 3.1). Augustus, Tiberius's predecessor on the imperial throne of the Roman empire, died in the year 14. So the great change in the life of Jesus mentioned above took place towards the end of the third decade of the first century. Luke is the only evangelist to relate that at that time Jesus was 'around thirty' (3.23). By then Judaea and Galilee had been under the control of the Roman authorities for almost a century. Little or nothing of the famous *pax Romana* could be detected there; there was almost constant unrest: riots, revolts and sometimes even skirmishes which developed into wars. The Jewish people was deeply divided. Some collaborated and others waged a guerilla war.

Jewish religion complicated the situation immensely. Did

belief in God call for opposition to the pagan rulers? The Zealots – enthusiasts for the Torah – answered this question in the affirmative and where possible sought to challenge the Romans and their Jewish minions. Other believers, like the Pharisees, were more moderate, but called for nothing less than a radical change in politics and the social situation. It seems likely that Jesus came from their circles. We can infer from the Gospels that his parents observed the commandments of the Torah closely. Thus the evangelist Luke comments that Jesus, fully in accord with the precepts of the Torah (Lev. 12.3), was circumcised on the eighth day (Luke 2.21); the commandments relating to cleanness were also taken seriously (Luke 2.22). In the Gospel of Mark Joseph is described as a 'righteous man', which means that he was known as someone who tried to live in accordance with the commandments of the Torah.

## A longing for liberation

Jesus lived in a Jewish world which passionately longed for liberation and redemption. The time seemed to be ripe for this. The past was recalled in words and writings. Every year the Jewish people celebrated the feast of Passover. Floods of pilgrims went to Jerusalem to commemorate the fact that long ago God had led Israel out of slavery in the land of Egypt 'with a strong hand and an outstretched arm' (Deut. 5.15). Every year hearts beat faster during the celebration of the Passover and the tension increased. God liberated the people from Egypt, and centuries later he brought the exiles back from Babylon to the promised land (Ps. 126). In the second century before our era God granted the Maccabees victory in their battle for their faith against their Syrian overlords. Almost another two centuries had passed since then, but the recollection of the successful opposition of the pious at this time was still fixed in people's memories.

The Jewish people had had the courage and the wisdom not only to recall the successes but also the defeats, the disappointments and the mistakes which had been made. Anyone who might have hoped that the Maccabean victory would be the beginning of a period of *shalom* – peace and justice – soon proved to be wrong. The division within the Jewish people did not diminish, but became even stronger. The successors to the Maccabees lost sight of the original ideals and strove for political power. They became oriental despots and came into conflict with their pious subjects. Towards the middle of the first century before the beginning of our era the internal oppositions became so great that different parties sent delegates to the Roman general Pompey, who was residing in Damascus, with a request for him to intervene. He did so in 63 BC, and thus introduced a period of Roman domination of the country which lasted for many centuries.

In the history of the Jewish people the disappointments constantly led to the rise of penitential movements. Among the pious, the blame for the failure was not sought primarily among others; above all they blamed themselves. They saw no other remedy for the evil than an even greater concentration on observing the commandments of the Torah. The origin of the Pharisaic movement, to which Jesus' parents belonged, is also to be sought in this spiritual atmosphere. Men and women who lived serious lives tried to put the commandments of the Torah into practice. They strove for purity and holiness. For this reason they lived as 'separated ones'. They sought support from one another and avoided all those whom they regarded as unclean because of their way of life.

Scripture played a central role in the life and thought of pious Jews. The present was illuminated and interpreted by the past. A stream of new writings was the direct consequence of this intensive and passionate investigation of scripture. Thus shortly after the coming of the Roman troops in 63 BC a remarkable book appeared, entitled Psalms of Solomon. The anonymous author was probably a scribe who belonged to Pharisaic circles. In the first chapters – called 'psalms' – he gives his critical commentary on the dramatic event that has recently taken place. In so doing he does not spare the descendants of the Maccabees, who in conflict with the precepts of the Torah had assumed the offices of both high priest and king of the Jewish people. At the end of his book the anonymous author recalls prophetic texts which had set their hope on a possible restoration of the dynasty of David (Isa. 11.1–10). We may rightly say that this pious writer had a bold vision of the future. Certainly the prophet Nathan had spoken of an eternal kingship of the dynasty of David (II Sam. 11–17), but since the beginning of the Babylonian captivity the throne of Jerusalem had no longer been occupied by a descendant of David. Now that the land of the Jews had become part of the mighty Roman empire, a fulfilment of the prophetic promises seemed to be further away than ever.

Times were changing, and therefore the ancient texts also needed to be read with new eyes. The prophetic expectations in scripture which arose in the period prior to the Babylonian exile were still directed towards the rehabilitation of the house of David – the son of David who now reigns does not walk in the footsteps of his illustrious predecessor, but a new son of David will soon come who will (Isa. 7.14; 11.1–10). When the author of the intertestamental work Psalms of Solomon set down his hopes and expectations in writing, the situation had drastically changed. The dynasty of David had disappeared from the throne in Jerusalem centuries before. Therefore the pious author confidently directs his gaze to the near future and sets his hope on the appearance of a new son of David, the Lord's anointed, the Messiah of Israel. The hour of the birth of messianic expectation is significant: it comes at a time when the future offered hardly any hope. Would the Messiah be able to drive out the Romans?

It is difficult to say how much influence the expectation of the coming of the Messiah had in the time of Jesus. At all events, the notion that the whole of the Jewish people were waiting tensely for the coming of the Messiah, which may enjoy some popularity in Christian circles, may confidently be assigned to

the realm of fable. That emerges among other things from the
writings of other pious men from the same period of Jewish
history. They are so much under the impact of the power of
forces in this world hostile to God that they expect little salvation from a possible return of the dynasty of David to the throne
in Jerusalem. They are pessimistic about the future of this world
and set their hope on the total dissolution of the old creation
and the coming of a new heaven and a new earth (Rev. 21.1).
These apocalyptists are not interested in the coming of the
Messiah. They hope for the moment when God will avenge himself and establish his power and his kingdom on a new earth
(Rev. 21.3).

## Jesus' baptism

Jesus grew up in this complex spiritual climate. He was one of
the many people who felt attracted to John the Baptist. According to the Gospel of Mark, John preached 'baptism of repentance for the forgiveness of sins' (Mark 1.4). Did Jesus really
need such a baptism? Was he sinful like everyone else? Since the
sinlessness of Jesus became an important pillar of the doctrine
of the atonement in later christological reflection, it is understandable that at a very early stage this question was answered
in the negative. According to the evangelist Matthew, John the
Baptist opposed Jesus' desire to be baptized by him: 'John
would have prevented him, saying, "I need to be baptized by
you, and do you come to me?" ' (Matt. 3.13).

Be this as it may, the baptism by John marks the beginning of
Jesus' public appearance. The evangelists tell of a voice from
heaven which calls him 'my beloved son', and of the Spirit of
God which descended like a dove upon him. Precisely what
happened can no longer be determined with certainty.
According to Mark and Luke the voice from heaven addressed
Jesus himself, 'You are my beloved son' (Mark 1.11; Luke
3.22), whereas in the Gospel of Matthew the bystanders are
addressed and their attention is drawn to Jesus with the words

'This is my beloved son' (Matt. 3.17). Nor is there unanimity about the coming of the Spirit of God. Matthew presupposes that John the Baptist saw the Spirit descending upon Jesus like a dove (Matt. 3.16), but Mark relates that Jesus himself saw it (Mark 1.10). Luke is silent here, but that raises another problem. Precisely what did John the Baptist or Jesus see? Is the descent of the Spirit of God a visible event? Luke is the only one to give an unequivocal answer to this question: 'And the Holy Spirit descended on him in bodily form as a dove' (Luke 3.22).

The evangelists were not eyewitnesses of the baptism of Jesus in the Jordan. They wrote their Gospels some decades later. They were not modern historians in search of an objective truth. Precisely what happened at the moment when Jesus was baptized in the Jordan? No clear answer to this question is possible. But something must have happened to him, since after that his life changed radically. From that moment on he knew himself to be called by God in a special way – the voice from heaven – and from that moment he proved to have special gifts and powers – the Spirit of God had descended on him.

## A hopeful beginning

That is how Jesus' public appearance began. He knew that he had been called by God and endowed with God's Spirit. He proved to be a charismatic who became a source of inspiration for his disciples and for all those who gladly heard him speak. He proclaimed the speedy coming of the kingdom of God (Mark 1.14–15). Clearly his view of the future was governed by apocalyptic images and notions. He was always very reticent over the question whether he could be the Messiah. Usually he required his conversation partners to be silent (Mark 8.30) and went on to speak of the coming of the Son of Man, who was known from apocalyptic literature (Mark 8.31–33). Jesus never put himself at the centre. When John the Baptist asked him from prison who he really was, Jesus answered with a reference to what he was doing: 'The blind receive their sight and the lame walk, lepers are cleansed and the deaf hear, and the dead are raised up, and the poor have good news preached to them' (Matt. 11.5).

After his baptism in the Jordan, Jesus went around the country for some time – the Synoptic Gospels suggest one year, but according to the Gospel of John it was at least three. His presence was felt to be refreshing and healing, a light in the darkness of everyday existence. He was concerned with the fate of people in need – including people in spiritual need. Here Jesus caused offence to pious people and came into conflict with some Pharisees. He gave priority to people who were in danger of getting lost: sinners and toll collectors (Mark 2.13–17; Matt. 21.28–32). Despite his Pharisaic background he was less concerned with the question whether contact with uncleanness could be a danger to his own efforts at a true and holy life. This religious unconcern was caused by his desire to devote himself heart and soul to other people. For him the spiritual and physical well-being of others came first. His life was stamped through and through with the characteristic of 'being there for others'.

## The dramatic end

The Gospel of John tells us that Jesus travelled to Jerusalem several times (2.13; 5.1; 7.14; 12.12). According to the Synoptic Gospels he only went up once to the city which plays such an important role in the history of the Jewish people. It is impossible to be certain which Gospel gives a historically reliable account of the event, and the question is not really relevant in connection with the topic of this book. The question why Jesus went up to Jerusalem is easier to answer. He always travelled as a pilgrim, and in so doing was observing the precepts of the Torah (Deut. 16.16–17).

The four evangelists are agreed that Jesus went on a pilgrimage to Jerusalem for the last time because he wanted to celebrate the Passover there. He arrived in a city full to bursting, where the tension was manifest. Every year the celebration of this festival in particular caused religious excitement. The remembrance of the exodus from Egypt in the distant past awakened a longing for liberation in the present. Over the years the Roman forces of occupation had learned their lesson, and they took precautionary measures so that the festivities would go off peacefully. Pontius Pilate, the procurator, came from his residence, Caesarea, with its fine location on the coast, bringing extra troops to crowded Jerusalem. He was prepared for anything and would not hesitate to maintain law and order with a firm hand. It was in this explosive atmosphere, full of tension and threat, that Jesus approached Jerusalem. The four evangelists have preserved the recollection that he did not enter the city unnoticed. Bystanders welcomed him as though he were a king (Mark 11.10). By this carefully prepared action, Jesus deliberately fixed attention on himself. His glorious entry alarmed both the Jewish leaders and the Roman authorities.

From that moment on Jesus' attitude changed. He very soon came into conflict with those who were responsible for conducting affairs in the temple (Mark 11.27–33). Nor was he silent in other discussions. He deliberately challenged his opponents (Mark 12.1–44). His striking entry into the city was followed – directly or a day later; the Gospels do not wholly agree on the timing (cf. Mark 11.11–25 with Matt. 21.12–22) – by a no less shocking scene in the temple. The temple authorities were provoked: did this Jesus of Nazareth think that in his criticism of the goings-on in the temple he could compare himself with the prophets from scripture?

Jesus was very popular among the people (Mark 11.18; 12.12; 14.2), but resistance to his behaviour grew in the circles of the Jewish leaders. Finally the decision was taken to arrest him and kill him (Mark 14.10–11). In Passover night, after Jesus had held the Seder meal with his companions, he was arrested in the garden of Gethsemane (Mark 14.43–52). The course of events did not surprise him, but he did not flee. He kept faith with himself and finally died as he had lived: fully dedicated to God and his fellow human beings. That is the reason for his dramatic wrestling in Gethsemane (Mark 15.32–42). It would have been possible for him to make another choice. He could easily have disappeared into the hills of Judaea in the darkness of the night. He would not have been the only one to seek timely rescue in that inhospitable region because the situation had become too hot for him. However, in the darkness of Gethsemane he realized that this way was closed to him. He sensed that God – his 'Abba' – required something else of him. Did he know why?

No convincing aswer to this question can be found in the Synoptic Gospels. It can be noted that Jesus did not go away. He remained in the Garden of Gethsemane and did not offer resistance when he was arrested. He accepted his fate and thought that he was acting in accordance with the will of God. Readers of the Gospels are confronted with a difficult dilemma. Do the stories about the event in Gethsemane need to be interpreted in the light of 'Jesus' knowledge' as that is emphasized in the Fourth Gospel, or is it wrong to burden the interpretation of the Synoptic Gospels with notions from the Gospel of John? The vast majority of exegetes have opted for the second possibility. According to the three Synoptic Gospels, in Gethsemane the man Jesus of Nazareth wrestled with the consequences of his task. He did not 'know' everything in advance. He was not the omniscient Son of God who knew and controlled the programme from beginning to end. That is the language and the thought-world of later dogma, but the New Testament authors do not yet use such concepts. No 'divine game' was played out in Gethsemane. Jesus did not put on a performance. At the end of his spiritual struggle he decided to follow God's way to the end. At this decisive moment he called God his 'Abba' and showed in practice that as a 'son' he was obedient to his Father.

Jesus of Nazareth died a cruel death on the cross at the beginning of the 30s of the first century. The sentence was carried out by Roman soldiers (Mark 15.39). It may be thought probable that this was not the first time in their careers that they had been part of an execution squad. Crucifixion was often used in the Roman empire. According to Roman law, runaway slaves and rebels had to be executed publicly in this abhorrent way. The Roman authorities expected that the sight of the long-drawn-out death struggle of those who were crucified would deter potential rebels and troublemakers and thus encourage law and order. Before the crucifixion, the condemned men were also tortured for some time by the soldiers. Jesus, too, suffered this terrible fate (Mark 15.16–39; John 19.23–24, 32–34). Execution of the sentence followed. A crucified man could not reckon on much sympathy or compassion from bystanders. Anyone who hung on the cross had not succeeded in his revolt and was easily made the butt of mockery and scorn. Popular favour can sometimes change quickly. This is also what happened to Jesus of Nazareth (Mark 15.29–32). Jesus was not stoned as one who had transgressed the Torah, but was crucified by Roman soldiers. Pontius Pilate had the text 'The king of the Jews' put on the cross on which Jesus was hung (Mark 15.26) with no other aim than to insult the Jewish leaders and ridicule the crucified man. His 'royal' entry ended ignominiously on the cross.

# 2

# Jesus on the Meaning of his Suffering

*According to plan?*

A monstrous alliance of Jewish leaders and Roman authorities of occupation was responsible for Jesus' death on the cross. Humanly speaking, this inspiring figure was taken from the earth much too early. However, anyone who reacts in this way is called to order by the Bible itself. The author of the Fourth Gospel emphasizes that there was no question of chance or a fatal combination of circumstances. The time was ripe: 'Now before the feast of the Passover, when Jesus knew that his hour had come to depart out of this world to the Father' (John 13.1). Jesus' career was 'planned' from beginning to end. Even his suffering and death took place under God's 'rule'.

In the Fourth Gospel Jesus is not the unwilling victim of the unexpected enmity of his Jewish contemporaries. His suffering does not surprise him, since he knows what to expect (John 13.1–3; 18.4). In the famous prologue the evangelist puts much emphasis on the pre-existence of the Word (John 1.1–18). As the Son, Jesus lay in the bosom of the Father (John 1.18). He knows God's plan. He is initiated into the mystery of God's love for human beings (John 3.16–17). The Son is sent by the Father, and as the one who comes 'from above' he can bear witness to what he has seen and heard 'above' (John 3.31–36).

Jesus' special 'spiritual affinity' with the Father meant that on earth Jesus alone knew the precise day and hour (John 2.4). For this reason, there is no mention in the Fourth Gospel of any hesitation on the part of Jesus. That is certainly the point of the story that the Synoptic Gospels relate about his wrestling in Gethsemane before his arrest (Mark 14.32–42). There is no longer a place for such an episode in the Gospel of John. Jesus knows that he cannot ask his Father to 'rescue him from this hour' (John 12.26).

In the passion narrative in the Gospel of John, Jesus is the one who is in charge and directs the dramatic event. At his arrest, soldiers and temple police shrink back and fall to the ground in terror when he makes himself known with the words 'I am he' (John 18.6). Jesus carries his own cross (John 19.17), and while he hangs on the cross he still seems to be in a condition to concern himself with his mother's future (John 19.25–27). Before the soldiers put the crucified men out of their suffering by breaking their legs (John 19.31–33), Jesus himself has already 'given up his spirit' (John 19.30).

## A revolution in scholarship

At the moment, dogma and exegesis are no longer speaking the same language. In classical christological dogma there was no doubt that Jesus had foreseen his suffering and death and had interpreted it as a 'perfect atonement for all our sins'. In dogmatic reflection the pre-existence of Jesus played an essential role and the Trinity formed the basis of the work of redemption by the Son of God.

For many centuries the Fourth Gospel played a key role in christological reflection. According to church tradition its author was none less than 'the Beloved Disciple', the key witness to crucial events in the life of Jesus (John 13.23; 19.25–27; 20.2). The words of such a person needed to be taken with utter seriousness and there was no doubt about their historical reliability.

Since the middle of the nineteenth century, far-reaching changes have taken place in the evaluation of the four Gospels. Historical criticism of the Bible has caused a 'revolution' which has also been extremely important for the christology of the

New Testament. It is neither possible nor necessary to sketch the debate in detail here, so I shall keep to the main points.

From the middle of the last century on, by far the majority of New Testament scholars have begun by assuming the priority of the Gospel of Mark. This Gospel, the shortest of the four, is regarded as the earliest and as an important source for the Gospels of Matthew and Luke. Now as the credentials of Mark rose, those of John declined. Anyone who wanted to paint a portrait of Jesus had to use Mark as a basis and certainly not John. The Fourth Evangelist was said not to be a reliable source. He was not a historian in the modern sense of the word. His work was that of a theologian who was giving his view some time after the death and resurrection of Jesus.

In the second half of the nineteenth cenutry the investigation of the life of Jesus occupied centre stage. This investigation was marked by unmistakable anti-dogmatic presuppositions. Exegetes no longer allowed church dogma to lay down the law; they hoped that, freed from its strait-jacket, they would rediscover the *authentic*, the historical, Jesus in the texts.

We are now living about a century later. A good deal has happened since then, but the debate about the historical Jesus does not yet seem to have lost any of its topicality. Much has changed, but it may be regarded as a constant that the Fourth Gospel has ceased to play a significant part in the discussion. At all events, Jesus was not the figure depicted by the evangelist John.

The Fourth Evangelist emphasizes Jesus' *knowledge*. The three Synoptic Gospels do not do so, or at all events do so to a considerably lesser degree. Whereas the Fourth Evangelist pays a good deal of attention to the unity between the Father and the Son, the three Synoptic Gospels leave no doubt that there is a difference between God and Jesus (Mark 10.18; 13.32). As a result, since the nineteenth century there has been far more emphasis on the humanity of Jesus. The Jesus who walked the earth was not the Christ of the doctrine of two natures who deliberately went to the cross on Golgotha to make his sacrifice in atonement for the sins of humankind. Jesus went around Galilee and Judaea, a man with special gifts, a healer and an exorcist, a creative exegete of the commandments of the Torah, proclaiming the imminent coming of the kingdom of God and in search of people who risked getting lost. He died a violent death on the cross. Had he expected this death?

## Prophecies after the event?

In the Synoptic Gospels, at least three times we have sayings of Jesus which can be understood as prophecies or announcements of his suffering and death (Mark 8.31; 9.31; 10.32–34). The content of these passages is roughly the same. I shall quote the shortest of the three:

> The Son of man will be delivered into the hands of men, and they will kill him; and when he is killed, after three days he will rise (Mark 9.31).

Did Jesus expect his death? Did he know what was in store for him? Does the classical dogma also find support in the Synoptic Gospels? One of the leading twentieth-century New Testament theologians, Rudolf Bultmann, gave a unambiguously negative answer to these questions. He described the announcements of Jesus' passion and death in Jerusalem mentioned above as *vaticinia ex eventu*, prophecies after the event. Only after Jesus' death and resurrection would the early Christian community have attributed these announcements to him. Since then there has been much discussion of this critical perspective. A consensus has not (yet) been reached, but exegetes who in general adopt a less critical standpoint still seem to think that Jesus' sayings about his possible suffering were altered after his death and resurrection by God so that they reflected the dramatic event better. That emerges above all from the third announcement, which contains a short summary of the whole of the passion narrative:

> Behold, we are going up to Jerusalem, and the Son of man
> will be delivered to the chief priests and the scribes, and they
> will condemn him to death, and deliver him to the Gentiles;
> and they will mock him, and spit upon him, and scourge him,
> and kill him; and after three days he will rise (Mark 10.33–
> 34).

It seems legitimate to conclude that this wording does not indicate the foreknowledge of Jesus, but the 'after-knowledge' of
the early Christian community. The same also goes for the first
announcement of the passion:

> And he began to teach them that the Son of man must suffer
> many things, and be rejected by the elders and the chief
> priests and the scribes, and be killed, and after three days rise
> again (Mark 8.31).Thus to a substantial degree the three
> announcements of the passion are indeed *vaticinia ex eventu*,
> prophecies after the event. In my view that does not mean
> that it is impossible for the nucleus of these words to go
> back to Jesus himself (see the wording of the second
> announcement). It is certainly not inconceivable that he
> expected his suffering and death in one way or another. That
> is also quite imaginable humanly speaking. He lived in an
> occupied land torn apart by tensions and conflicts. His words
> and actions attracted wide attention. He went on pilgrimage
> to Jerusalem at a time, the feast of Passover, when the long-
> ing for liberation was again reaching a climax.

The first announcement of the passion speaks of 'must'.
Many exegetes interpret this as a divine 'must', and therefore
conclude that it must be an interpretation after the event. But it
is also possible to interpret this 'must' in terms of inevitability.
The circumstances were such that it was quite conceivable that
Jesus would have to suffer in Jerusalem.

*'For many'*

The question whether Jesus did not just foresee his suffering but also attached significance to it comes to a head in a certain number of passages in the passion narrative in the Synoptic Gospels. We cannot know precisely what Jesus said or thought. His words are written in Greek, whereas he spoke Aramaic. Thus someone – possibly the evangelist – has translated them. We see all that we know of Jesus through tinted spectacles: his actions, his words and also his thoughts. Who ever knows what someone else is really thinking? The first text that calls for attention functions in the Gospel of Mark as an introduction to the passion narrative:

> And whoever would be first among you must be slave of all. For the Son of man also came not to be served but to serve, and to give his life as a ransom for many (Mark 10.44–45).

A number of aspects of this text call for our attention. First, a direct link is made between Jesus' being a servant and the attitude of his followers. This is in flagrant contradiction to the wishes of the disciples, which are focussed on places of honour in the kingdom of God (Mark 10.37). In the context of the saying of Jesus in the Gospel, the emphasis is not on the christology, but a christological statement is made to serve ethics: the disciples must learn that they have to behave in a different way from that customary in society. They are not rulers but servants, just as Jesus also lived as a 'servant'. This interpretation is supported by the version which is to be found in the Gospel of Luke:

> But not so with you; rather let the greatest among you become as the youngest, and the leader as one who serves. For which is the greater, one who sits at table or one who serves? Is not the one who sits at table? But I am among you as one who serves (Luke 22.26–27).

Jesus' life can be portrayed as a 'life of service', as a life in the service of others, a life 'for others'. As he lived, so he died. Therefore his suffering and death can be called a suffering and death 'for others'. The passage from the Gospel of Mark quoted earlier must also be understood in this spirit: 'and give his life a ransom for many' (Mark 10.45). It remains difficult to say whether here we have words of Jesus or a subsequent interpretation by the community. The latter seems more probable than the former. However, that does not mean that Jesus could not have interpreted his own suffering and death in the sense of a dying 'for many'. It seems legitimate to suppose that he in fact did so. That could at least be inferred from the words which he spoke in connection with the customary actions of the Jewish Seder meal. By that I mean those texts which in the church and theology are usually called the eucharistic words of institution. The question is particularly complicated and a large number of books have already been written about it. Again I shall deliberately keep to the main points.

The Synoptic Gospels leave no doubt that Jesus' last meal with his disciples was a Seder meal. During this meal, at which the Exodus from Egypt was remembered with an emphasis on the approaching liberation from oppression, Jesus added some words about himself to the customary 'liturgy'.

Much attention has been paid in exegetical literature to the fact that we actually have two traditions with eucharistic words of institution. On the one hand, there are the sayings in the Gospels of Mark and Matthew, which show a strong affinity with each other (Mark 14.22–25; Matt. 26.26–29); on the other, there are the passages in the Gospel of Luke and Paul's first letter to the community of Corinth (Luke 22.14–20; I Cor. 11.23–25). The differences between the two traditions are considerable. Thus the passages in Luke and Paul contain an unmistakable instruction for the community to repeat the ritual, 'Do this in memory of me' (Luke 22.19; I Cor. 11.24–25), whereas this command is missing from the Gospels of Mark and Matthew. Both evangelists relate the event during Jesus' last supper with his disciples as a facet of the passion narrative and do not make any particular links with possible usages in the later community. Both evangelists seem particularly matter-of-fact in their accounts.

In my view the words in the Gospels of Mark and Matthew stand closer to the past than the passages in the Gospel of Luke and Paul's letter. However, that does not mean that we now know precisely what Jesus said and did. While he was breaking and passing round the bread – the *mazzoth* – he associated it with his own fate: 'This is my body.' The same thing happened as a cup of wine was being passed round: 'This is my blood of the covenant.' It is not impossible that this was all that he said, and that the words 'shed for many' are already a later addition by the early Christian community, which needed to interpret the words in more detail. Be this as it may, what does the expression 'my blood of the covenant' mean? In all probability, here Jesus was alluding to the remarkable ritual which according to Exodus 24 took place during the making of the covenant between God and the people of Israel. In this ritual there is still no mention at all of blood which brings about reconciliation between God and human beings. When the people of Israel took upon themselves the obligations of the covenant, they were sprinkled with blood by Moses. Evidently the blood sealed their readiness to submit to the demands which the covenant with God entailed.

If it is true that the Gospels of Mark and Matthew bring us closest to Jesus' original words, then they confront us with a mystery which is difficult to fathom. What did Jesus intend? It certainly seems as if we may not isolate this meal from the other meals which Jesus held with his disciples and others (e.g. Mark 6.30–44; 8.1–10). A shared meal was an important event in the Jewish world. Eating together at table created a bond which could prove to be close and even indissoluble. Thus Jesus himself ate with sinners and toll collectors, and with outcasts who lived like sheep without a shepherd (Mark 2.15–17). In these shared meals we find once again an indication that he did not live for himself but 'for others'. This 'line' in his life comes to a climax during the last supper with his disciples. In the 'signs' of bread and wine he forges a bond with them which is sealed in his 'blood of the covenant'. That here we are a long way from any kind of sacrificial rituals may be evident from the notable fact that Jesus did not compare himself in any way to the Passover lamb. Moreover the lamb had no function as a sacrificial animal. The Passover lamb was indeed slaughtered in the temple, but it was not offered on the altar afterwards. It was taken home, there to be prepared as the main course of the Seder meal.

## 'My God, my God . . .'

One last aspect needs to be added to what has already been said. Jesus interpreted his own fate in the light of the Old Testament–Jewish tradition about the suffering of the righteous. According to the evangelist Mark, on the cross Jesus said 'Eloi, eloi, lama sabacthani' (Mark 15.3–4). In the distress of death he cried out words taken from one of the psalms in which a suffering righteous man turns to God in anguish and despair: 'My God, my God, why have you forsaken me?' (Ps. 22.1).

These words echo despair, but also hope. In Psalm 22 a change suddenly takes place. The poet is in great distress, but nevertheless he trusts in the nearness of God: 'But you, Lord, be not far off! You who are my help, hasten to my aid' (Ps. 22.19). His trust is not put to shame, because later he adds in exultation, 'You have heard me!' (Ps. 22.24). Those who trust in God and walk in the ways of the Lord – and the righteous man differs from others in doing this – will be confronted with suffering, but may know at the same time that God does not lose sight of them. Read against this background, the last words of Jesus no longer simply and solely indicate his solitude and perplexity, but also echo hope and trust in God. God never forsakes his righteous utterly.

# 3

# The Question of God

*God raised him from the dead*

Jesus' death on the cross was the dramatic end to the life of an inspired man. He did not attempt to avoid the danger which threatened in Gethsemane, by taking refuge in the solitary and inhospitable hills of Judaea. He had come to realize that it was the will of God that he should not oppose evil. Anyone who reads the passion narratives in the Gospels will involuntarily be overcome by a mixture of feelings. The way in which Jesus meets his approaching suffering is impressive and moving. For his disciples his arrest proves to be the signal to make their escape (Mark 14.30). He goes to meet his end abandoned by all. He provokes his interrogators by his silence (Mark 14.60–61; 15.4). He sows confusion with his enigmatic answers. In fact neither the Jewish nor the Roman authorities knew what to do with him and condemned him to death without giving clear grounds for the sentence (Mark 14.53–65; 15.1–5).

Therefore the account of Jesus' passion provokes both bewilderment and anger. An innocent man is put to death. He is the victim of the realism and cynicism of those in power, who do not hesitate to sacrifice a human life because they think that necessary or desirable (John 11.50–51). Finally, the death of Jesus on the cross arouses incomprehension and perplexity. Why does God not intervene? Why does God allow his 'beloved son', the 'apple of his eye', the man whom he had chosen to be the bearer of his Spirit, to be treated like that?

Jesus dies with the words of a psalmist on his lips: 'My God,

my God, why have you forsaken me?' (Mark 15.34). Is this the
sign of his despair and desperation? Does he feel forsaken by his
God, his 'Abba'? It may be inferred from the fact that Jesus
made these particular words his own that he recognized himself
in the wrestling of the psalmist (Ps. 22.1). Jesus was faithful to
God. His knowledge of scripture and tradition will have taught
him that the career of a righteous man can be full of stumbling
blocks and obstacles. Because of his faithfulness to God he was
persecuted, tortured and killed. However, the psalm also shows
that the poet may in turn experience the faithfulness of God
(Ps. 22.22). Jesus prays the beginning of the psalm. He too will
also have known persecution. So we may conclude that something more than simply despair and desperation is expressed in
his cry on the cross.

The poet of Psalm 22 is saved from the danger of death in
which he found himself. Suddenly he interrupts his lament and
exclaims: 'You have answered me' (Ps. 22.22). History does not
repeat itself. Jesus dies on the cross. His body is put in a tomb
(Mark 15.42–47). Did he cry out in vain? Was his faith in God
put to shame? The account of Jesus' passion makes a deep
impression because it is a story of all times. As so often, this
time, too, the wicked powers seem to be stronger than a human
being with ideals of love, justice and *shalom*. Should not God
himself be capable of fighting against evil?

The story takes an unexpected turn. Some women from the
group of Jesus' disciples discover soon afterwards that something has happened which initially they find impossible to
understand. According to the Gospel of Mark this discovery
simply gave rise to terror and dismay (Mark 16.1–8). What had
happened?

It is certainly impossible to give a clear answer to this
question. To the present day the Christian church confesses with
the words of the Apostles' Creed that Jesus Christ 'rose again on
the third day from the dead'. For centuries few people had
difficulty in believing that Jesus' resurrection really happened.
The stories in the Gospels were thought to be historically quite

trustworthy: on Easter morning the tomb was really empty and even the 'doubting' Thomas was convinced when he was invited to put his fingers into the wounds in the body of the risen Lord where the signs of his suffering were still visible (John 20.24–29). A more realistic idea of things is hardly possible. Jesus is alive. He has returned from death to life.

Honesty compels us to recognize that nowadays many people in the church find it difficult to believe in the reality of Easter. That is because the modern picture of the world leaves little or no room for 'miracle' – an event which cannot find any place in a scientific approach to reality. However, the difficulties are also caused by the complexity of the resurrection narratives in the four Gospels. These narratives differ from one another at so many points that it is impossible to sketch a clear picture of the event. Mary Magdalene, accompanied by some other women, sees that Jesus is no longer where they expected him: in the tomb. God has raised the crucified Jesus from the dead (Mark 16.6).

An obvious question is: if he is no longer in the tomb, where is he? According to the account in the Gospel of Mark Jesus has gone ahead of his disciples to Galilee. There they will see him (Mark 16.7). This evangelist does not say whether this promise was fulfilled, but his colleague Matthew does. On a mountain in Galilee Jesus bids farewell to his disciples after commanding them to go out on a mission (Matt. 28.16–20). In the Gospel of Luke, after Easter the focus is no longer on Galilee. The 'appearances' of Jesus take place exclusively in Jerusalem or in the immediate environs of the city (Luke 24.13–49). There Jesus bids farewell to his followers at a meal: 'And when he had said this, as they were looking on, he was lifted up, and a cloud took him out of their sight' (Acts 1.9).

The Fourth Gospel makes things even more complicated. Much attention is paid to the encounter between Jesus and Mary of Magdala (John 20.11–18). Moreover it is striking that Easter, Ascension and Pentecost seem to fall on one and the same day (John 20.17,22). Although it is not stated in so many words, there seems every reason to suppose that according to the Fourth Gospel, too, the appearances of Jesus took place primarily in Jerusalem. Only in the closing chapter is there mention of an encounter in Galilee. However, presumably this chapter was added later. To give simply one argument: the closing verses of Chapter 20 are unmistakably intended to be the end of the Fourth Gospel as a whole (John 20.30–31).

The Gospels were written some decades after Easter. It is by no means my intention to keep pestering readers with this fact, but we do need to remember it when reading the Gospel texts. Precisely what happened completely escapes our perception. We look at the past through the eyes of the evangelists and their sources. They did not intend to write a historical account in the modern sense of the word. In their stories about Jesus they were expressing their faith. So they also wrote accounts of the resurrection of Jesus. On the basis of their experiences, they had arrived at the insight that God had nevertheless been faithful to the crucified Jesus, his 'beloved son', the righteous sufferer. Certainly he had died on the cross, but God had then raised him from the dead.

What are we to think of this? To begin with I must state that theology – in the strict sense of the word, as 'teaching about God' – precedes christology. With its belief in the resurrection of Jesus, the early Christian community was first of all confessing its faith in the God of Israel. Very much in line with the Old Testament Jewish tradition, it lived by the conviction that history is guided by God. But that does not mean that all questions are permanently solved. Quite the contrary, since those who believe in God's guidance come up against insoluble questions. The prophet who is called 'Second Isaiah' already knew this: 'Truly you are a God who hides yourself, the God of Israel, a redeemer' (Isa. 45.15). Hiddenness and redemption, as it were in one breath – the same almost intolerable tension can also be seen in the Christian confession of the crucified man who was raised by God from the dead (I Cor. 15.3–4).

The resurrection stories teach that Jesus appeared exclusively to people who were prepared to follow him. Belief in God's new creative action evidently also creates a renewed form of humanity. Therefore it is legitimate to conclude that Jesus 'rises' in those who venture to follow his way. Thus he continues to 'live', not only in the memory but also in our time. The Spirit of God which inspired him did not disappear with him, but to the present day inspires anyone who follows him on God's way.

## From Jesus to Jesus Christ

In scholarly literature a distinction is usually made between 'Jesus before Easter and 'Jesus after Easter', or between the historical Jesus and the proclaimed, kerygmatic Christ. That distinction was created by Easter. During his life on earth Jesus did not make himself the centre of his preaching, but put all the emphasis on the imminent coming of the kingdom of heaven. However, after Easter, Jesus Christ became the centre of christological reflection in the early Christian community. The one who proclaimed the approaching kingdom of God himself becomes the content of the proclamation in the Christian community.

The writings in the New Testament show how quickly these christological developments took place in the first century of church history. Above all they made the Gospels complicated writings. The Gospels contain recollections of 'Jesus before Easter', but these recollections are always coloured by new views of the past which came into being as a result of belief in 'Jesus after Easter'. Through its belief in the resurrection of the crucified Jesus by God, the early Christian community in fact knew more than 'Jesus before Easter'. The evangelists projected knowledge that they had only acquired later on to their description of the life of 'Jesus before Easter'.

It is a complicated business. The difference between 'Jesus before Easter' and 'Jesus after Easter' cannot be trivialized. The resurrection of the crucified Jesus by God created such a new situation that it is no exaggeration to describe it as a break, an abyss, discontinuity. At the same time, however, it is wrong to give the impression that there can no longer be any question of any continuity. God raised Jesus, the crucified, suffering righteous man, from death. This continuity between 'Jesus before Easter' and 'Jesus after Easter' is also expressed in the fact that christological reflection within the early community began with Jesus' last words on the cross. In Jerusalem, gradually the suspicion arose within the community that Jesus' career had to be understood in the light of the Old Testament Jewish tradition about the righteous sufferer. What was initially a suspicion developed into a conviction. That was how he died. After Easter the early Christian community could make this conviction its own.

The suffering of the righteous had also already raised many questions in the past: questions about human beings, but also questions about God, about his faithfulness and his love. Why was it the righteous who had to suffer? On Golgotha history seemed to be repeating itself. God maintained a disturbing and incomprehensible silence. God did not intervene. Had God turned away? Was he hiding himself from the suffering of his righteous? Easter taught that at all events God had to be spoken of in a complex way: 'Truly you are a God who hides yourself, the God of Israel, a redeemer.'

## God and human suffering

The lament of the poet of Psalm 22 confronts us with the problem of human suffering. Why do people suffer? Is there an explanation or is suffering a necessary evil, part of being human? The Bible is not satisfied with the second alternative. It does not deny or trivialize human suffering. On the contrary, the reality of human suffering is taken completely seriously, with the result that the Old Testament Jewish tradition engages in a passionate search for its origin and cause. Anyone who tries to chart the different traces will again discover that the Bible does not give simple answers to these questions.

According to the creation story in Genesis, the origin of suffering has to be sought in human beings themselves. They cannot point a finger accusingly at God; human beings themselves are responsible for their own suffering and death. The creation began in a promising way. The first chapter of the Bible is one great hymn of praise to a *good* creation (Gen. 1). On the sixth day human beings appear on the scene: 'And God created the human being after his image; after God's image he created the human being, male and female he created them' (Gen. 1.27). Initially everything seemed to be going in accordance with God's wishes: the world was a paradise. However, sadly a dangerous serpent entered this paradise. God had not created human beings as puppets, but as beings capable of thought, who could consciously choose between good and evil. Human freedom is the cause of what the church and theology came to call 'the Fall'. Human beings choose and choose wrongly. At that moment the human being disobeys God's commandment and deserves to be punished with death (Gen. 2.17). Paradise lies in the past (Gen. 3.1–24).

The disobedience of Adam and Eve, the 'Fall', results in the alienation of human beings from God. Since then the ways of God and human beings have no longer run parallel. If the discussion is to be understood properly, at this point a brief incidental remark needs to be made. In the Jewish tradition the Genesis story of the Fall is not usually painted in dark colours. Human beings are disobedient to God's command, but that does not mean that the gulf between God and human beings cannot be bridged. God constantly seeks human beings out again and successively makes a covenant with Noah (Gen. 9.8–17), with Abraham (Gen. 12.1–9; 17.1–27) and finally with the people of Israel (Ex. 19.1–25). The loss of paradise is serious, but not an irrevocable catastrophe. After being driven out of paradise, human beings begin to till the ground (Gen. 3.23), and according to an old Jewish view that means that people in all their frailty set to work on the consummation of the creation which God has begun.

As I have remarked, the Christian tradition reads the story of the 'Fall' in a much more negative way. The reason for that is that already at an early stage of church history it was interpreted 'christologically'. Adam and Eve's 'Fall' was even said to have led to hostility to God, so great that reconciliation or atonement was needed. Nothing more could be expected of 'fallen human beings' and therefore from an early stage of Christian tradition the saying 'I will put enmity between you and the woman, and between your seed and her seed; he shall bruise your head, and you shall bruise his heel' (Gen. 3.15) was read as a first reference to the coming of the Messiah who would crush the serpent's head, overcome death and bring about reconciliation between God and humankind.

### 'He will not be angry for ever . . .'

The Old Testament is an extremely variegated book. It may begin with the account of creation and the 'Fall', but that does not mean that this theological view is characteristic of the whole of the Old Testament. Certainly the prophets, too, speak of sin and guilt. They do not see the deportation of the people of Israel as a caprice of fate, but as God's punishment for the sins of the people. For this reason the godless usurper Nebuchadnezzar from Babylon can be called 'God's servant' by the prophet Jeremiah (27.6). The powerful king is in fact no more or no less than an instrument in the hand of the God of Israel. Prophets warn the people of God's punishment and are not afraid also to interpret world history in these terms.

However, that is not the whole story. One of the psalmists expressed the mystery of God's love and faithfulness like this:

The Lord is merciful and gracious,
slow to anger and abounding in steadfast love.
He will not always chide,
nor will he keep his anger for ever.
He does not deal with us according to our sins,

nor requite us according to our iniquities.
For as the heavens are high above the earth,
so great is his steadfast love
towards those who fear him (Ps. 103.8–11).

The Bible is very variegated and God has many 'faces'. God's punishment can be fearful, but it also knows a limit. God's anger is terrible, but it does not last for ever. Measured by human standards God is in a mysterious way 'incalculable'. He does not always remain the same, but changes when he wants to and thinks it necessary. Another prophet experienced that. In scholarly literature he is called 'Second Isaiah'. This prophet, the author of Isaiah 40–55, lived at the end of the Babylonian exile. Meanwhile the balance of power in the Near East had changed decisively. The Babylonians were defeated by the Persians under the leadership of their king Cyrus. This new usurper practised a different policy towards his subject peoples. He gave the exiles in his territories permission to return home to their own cities and villages. Was Cyrus more philanthropic than his predecessors? That does not seem very likely. There was no question of his withdrawing from the occupied territories. The land of Israel did not become an independent state, and the dynasty of David did not return to the throne of Jerusalem. Cyrus had simply found a different method of maintaining his power in the territories occupied by his armies. Yet Second Isaiah gives the Persian king an unparalleled honorific title: 'the Lord's anointed' (Isa. 45.1). Cyrus became a messianic figure because he gave the Jewish people permission to return to the promised land and rebuild the temple. The punishment now lay in the past. A new exodus began, and the exiles again set out for the promised land.

God's ways are complex and mysterious. The Second Isaiah can clearly live with that mystery. He attributes so much power and authority to God that he puts not only good in the divine hands but also evil: 'I am the Lord, and there is no other. I form light and create darkness, I make weal and create woe, I am the

Lord who do all these things' (Isa. 45.6–7). Darkness and disaster are terrifying, but they are always best kept in God's hands. The Bible continues to be preoccupied with the question of the cause of human suffering. The prophet who has been given the name 'Second Isaiah' is not afraid of drawing conclusions from his faith in the God of Israel: 'I am the Lord, and there is no other.' The vulnerability and capriciousness of human existence does not disappear, but is put in a new perspective. Sometimes it looks as if God hides himself and does not want to hear, or does not usually hear, the complaints of his people. At such a moment of godforsakenness the hidden God can suddenly prove to be the Redeemer: 'Truly, you are a God who hides yourself, the God of Israel, a redeemer' (Isa. 45.15).

## The righteous sufferer

Why do human beings have to suffer and die? Anyone who believes in one God can easily be perplexed by this question. That is also evident from the answers which are formulated in the Bible. On the whole there is no question of a 'dogmatic' unity and unanimity. Monotheism is a 'game' with no more than two players, God and human beings. The origin of evil and human suffering cannot be sought outside these two players. Prophets confront human beings with their guilt towards God. That is why human beings suffer, and that is why the people of Israel was led into captivity.

But are human begins really always guilty? Job opposes this notion with all his might. He knows that he is righteous and therefore he cannot simply accept the disasters with which he is tried. They cannot be a punishment for his sins, since he refuses to see himself as a sinful man.

In the history of the Jewish people the lament of the righteous Job becomes increasingly relevant. Those who are righteous – in other words, those who observe the commandments of the Torah – discover that they are not free of suffering in this world. On the contrary, experience teaches that obedience to the commandments has consequences, and can sometimes even result in death. This was the experience of the pious in the second century before our era when they refused to follow the trend at the time of the radical religious reforms carried out by the Syrian ruler Antiochus IV Epiphanes and his Jewish collaborators. Appealing to God's covenant, they wanted to remain faithful to the commandments of the Torah despite all threats and tortures. They were persecuted and killed. Because of their zeal for the Torah, they died as martyrs. They were ready to put their own lives at risk, because they had other priorities. They thought that obedience to the Torah was more important than saving their own lives.

Thus, slowly but surely, in the period around the beginning of our era the tradition of the suffering righteous arose. Is this suffering also to be interpreted as 'suffering for others'? This question arises almost automatically, but it is difficult to give an answer in a few words. Beyond question, in this context attention also needs to be paid to the figure of the suffering servant of the Lord in the book of Second Isaiah. This 'servant', too, seems to be a righteous man. He suffers because he is faithful. His suffering has meaning for others. Moreover, here too we have the notion that this suffering does not lie outside God. Does God want the servant to suffer? It is difficult to answer this question with an unambiguous 'yes' or 'no'. When reacting we need to reflect that this text too was written by Second Isaiah, the same prophet who earlier put both good and evil in God's hands.

In the early Jewish tradition, certainly under the impact of the persecutions at the time of the Maccabees, increasing attention was paid to the special character of the suffering of the righteous, and people were also bold enough to give this suffering a meaning. That is clear, for example, from the re-interpretation of the well-known story in Genesis 22. According to the current interpretation of this story Abraham's faith was put to the test and Isaac simply played an incidental role. In Jewish exegesis, the spotlight has been increasingly put on Isaac.

He is the one who is ready to take suffering upon himself. That makes him the symbol of the righteous sufferer *par excellence*. His readiness for sacrifice becomes a source of inspiration for others and consequently takes on an 'exemplary' character. Without going into this further here, I would refer to the Jewish tradition, in which it is said that every generation has its righteous.

## Jesus' suffering

We can understand how already in the first years of the existence of the early Christian community, the need was felt to provide a consecutive survey of the recent, dramatic events. Of course the facts as such were still fresh in the memory of those who had experienced them. But the question of the precise meaning of what had happened needed to be seen and, if possible, given an answer. In itself, Jesus' journey to Jerusalem was neither strange nor unique. Every year many people went up from Galilee to Jerusalem on the occasion of the great pilgrimage festivals. Jesus was one of them. In so doing he was fulfilling an obligation which was prescribed by the Torah. Did the events in Jerusalem overwhelm him? Did they surprise him and disconcert him? Thus relatively soon after the suffering and death of Jesus a more or less consecutive account was composed which formed the basis of the passion narratives in the Gospels. We may see this original passion narrative as the first step in the long course of christological reflection. The time of the great and authoritative christological dogmas is still far away. Still, the members of the early Christian community in Jerusalem were in a unique position. They had either been present at the event or had followed it at a distance. However, while they were eyewitnesses, they had understood little. Disciples fell asleep (Mark 14.40), took flight (14.50) and denied their teacher (14.66–72): women did their duty towards their beloved dead master (16.1) and reacted to their discovery of the empty tomb with terror and bewilderment (16.1–8).

Can a 'good' word be said about the death of Jesus? In the Roman world, death on the cross was seen as a disgrace. At the time of Jesus such an execution was viewed in different ways. A text could be found in the Torah which interpreted hanging on the wood as a curse by God (Deut. 21.23 – thus also Paul in Gal. 3.13), but on the other hand, over the course of years this fate had befallen a large number of Jews who had come to oppose the occupying forces out of conviction. Death on the cross could therefore also be seen as a symbol of loyalty to God's command.

There were various eyewitnesses to the suffering and death of Jesus within the early Christian community in Jerusalem. It was natural that they should try to understand it in the light of scripture and tradition. Therefore the original passion narrative is more than simply a historical account. It is not 'objective', but has the character of a theological 'chronicle'. It is not about the facts as such, but about the theological relevance of these facts. Why did Jesus die on the cross? Why did this 'righteous' man meet with this fate?

To answer this question the early Christian community investigated scripture and tradition and in so doing came upon the significant motif of the righteous sufferer. In the passion narrative there are many quotations from and allusions to the Old Testament psalms of suffering (Psalms 22; 27; 40; 41; 68; 71), the songs of the suffering servant of the Lord (Isa. 53), and certain passages in the inter-testamental writing known as the Wisdom of Solomon (chapters 2 and 5). Here is an impressive quotation from this work. The words are spoken by the enemies of an anonymous righteous man. But they could just as well also have been spoken by the Jewish leaders who were furious at the actions of Jesus:

Let us lie in wait for the righteous man,
because he is inconvenient to us
and opposes our actions;
he reproaches us for sins against the law,

and accuses us of sins against our training.
He professes to have knowledge of God,
and calls himself a child of the Lord.
He became to us a reproof of our thoughts;
the very sight of him is a burden to us,
because his manner of life is unlike that of others,
and his ways are strange.
We are considered by him as something base,
and he avoids our ways as unclean;
he calls the last end of the righteous happy,
and boasts that God is his father.
Let us see if his words are true,
and let us test what will happen at the end of his life;
for if the righteous man is God's son,
he will help him,
and will deliver him from the hand of his adversaries.
Let us test him with insult and torture,
that we may find out how gentle he is,
and make trial of his forbearance.
Let us condemn him to a shameful death,
for, according to what he says,
he will be protected (Wisdom 2.12–20).

# 4

# Paul's View

## A *chronological problem*

Developments in human thought can be described when the age of relevant sources can be established with a certain degree of probability. In addition it is necessary to gain some insight into the interrelationship of the sources. Here New Testament scholarship does not face an easy task.

In the second half of the fourth century, the New Testament assumed an extent which began to be regarded as 'canonical'. In the previous period there were deep differences of opinion over various writings. A certain consensus in the church took some time to develop. As the canon was formed, the division between canonical and non-canonical works was not based on the criterion of the date of composition of the individual writings; the New Testament was arranged thematically. The four Gospels describe the life of Jesus; they are followed by the Acts of the Apostles, central to which is the origin of the early Christian church; the heading after that is 'letters' – most of them under the name of the apostle Paul. This is a logical development: the letters give an impression of how things were going within a number of communities. Finally the New Testament was concluded by the Revelation of John, in which readers are confronted with visions of the future.

The fact that according to present-day scholarship the 'canonical' division of the New Testament does not run parallel to an order based on the date of composition of the individual writings causes confusion. Thus while the four Gospels come first, they cannot be counted among the earliest writings in the

New Testament. Beyond doubt the earliest writings are the letters of the apostle Paul. But this statement too needs to be qualified. It is not absolutely certain that all the letters which bear Paul's name were really written by him. We can be sure only about seven epistles: Paul wrote to the communities of Rome and Corinth (two letters), to the Galatians, the Thessalonians (only the first letter) and the Philippians, and finally he also wrote the short letter to Philemon. New Testament scholars are not agreed over the remaining 'Pauline' writings. Despite differences in content, the letters to the communities of Colossae and Ephesus still show so much affinity to the 'authentic' letters of Paul that they are usually attributed to one of Paul's fellow workers (for example Timothy or Silvanus). As for the rest of the 'Pauline' letters – the second letter to the community of Thessalonica, the two letters to Timothy and the letter to Titus – scholars have come to the conclusion that these were written significantly later, presumably by a representative of the 'school of Paul'. Those investigating the apostle's theological views need to take account of this.

Paul wrote his letters at the end of the 40s and during the 50s of the first century. Between the suffering and death of Jesus and the composition of these writings lies a period of hardly more than twenty years. The four Gospels were completed later: the Gospel of Mark shortly before or shortly after the destruction of the temple in AD 70; Matthew, Luke and John not before the middle of the 80s. That means that all four Gospels are further removed from the dramatic event in Jerusalem than the letters of Paul. Is the apostle to the Gentiles therefore the most reliable witness? It might perhaps seem natural to draw this conclusion, but if we do, we may easily find ourselves on a false trail. It must be doubted whether the four evangelists were eye-witnesses. However, it is also more or less certain that Paul, too, never met Jesus during his lifetime. As representatives of a subsequent generation of disciples of Jesus, the four evangelists were dependent on both oral and written sources (Luke 4.1–4). The apostle Paul was writing some decades earlier, but he too based his work on the accounts of others. He does not say this often, but sometimes he openly acknowledges it (I Cor. 11.23; 15.3).

## Biographical notes

Paul wrote complicated letters. The result was that at a very early stage in church history his writings became food for dogmatic theologians. We may ask whether he himself would have been very happy with this development. The literature he left behind consists exclusively of letters and contains no dogmatic treatises. Even his letter to the community of Rome, generally regarded as the most systematic of his epistles, contains primarily theological 'fragments' and is certainly not well-rounded systematic reflection on the significance of the suffering and death of Jesus Christ. Above all Paul was a practical man. He was concerned about the situation in the community. With all the acuteness and creativity that he possessed, he sought solutions to problems that had arisen and possibilities of ending conflicts between parties. Paul was a true bridge-builder. There were tensions within many communities: between masters and slaves; between men and women; but above all between members with a Jewish background and others who were of pagan origin. What was special about Paul was that he was better than anyone else at putting himself in this situation. That will have been the reason why his letters were preserved and disseminated. The apostle had something to say. Doubtless not everyone will have agreed with him. His ideas will have given rise to new differences of opinion, but what he wrote in his letters was always worth reflecting on.

Paul had a complicated, variegated background. It is not necessary to describe it all in detail in this book, so I shall content myself with some of the most important biographical information. Paul was proud of his Jewish origin (Phil. 3.5–8). Many years after the event near Damascus which was so important for his life, he boasts of having been 'extremely zealous for the traditions of my fathers' (Gal. 1.14). It may perhaps seem surprising, but he is not ashamed that his 'former life in Judaism' led him to 'persecute the church of God violently'. In his zeal he had even gone so far as to try to 'exterminate it' (Gal. 1.13).

The picture of Paul as a pious Pharisee burning with zeal is impressive, but it is only one side of this many-sided personality. Paul was a man of two cultures. He himself does not write much about it, but Luke tells us that the apostle came from Tarsus in Cilicia and that he was trained in Jerusalem by the Pharisaic scribe Gamaliel, who was a key figure at that time (Acts 22.1–3). It is worth dwelling on this fact for a moment. Paul was a Diaspora Jew. At that time his birthplace enjoyed a high reputation. Tarsus, in the centre of Asia Minor, was not only an important trading city but was also regarded as a centre of Graeco-Hellenistic wisdom. What happens to a person when he or she moves from one culture to another which is totally different? Experience tells us that in such cases it is no exaggeration to speak of a culture shock. So what happened to Paul when he arrived in Jerusalem? He had grown up in a Graeco-Roman city with temples dedicated to different gods, with busy market-places, with philosophical schools and gymnasia where athletes engaged in sport naked, in accordance with the custom of the time. In the middle of all the public buildings and private houses perhaps somewhere there was an unobtrusive small building which served as a synagogue. At regular times the Jews from the city would come there to say their prayers and to read scripture. As a Diaspora Jew Paul was accustomed to being an exception. His journey to Jerusalem shows that he was aware of his Jewishness and that he wanted to know more about the Torah. Once he arrived in Jerusalem, a new world must have opened up for him. Outwardly, the city might not perhaps have seemed too different from Tarsus. Since the reign of king Herod, Jerusalem had been rapidly transformed into a city which with its broad, straight streets met the architectural requirements of the Graeco-Roman world. But Jerusalem differed from all other cities. Its silhouette was completely dominated by the awe-inspiring temple complex. For a Diaspora Jew like Paul, it must have been a moving experience to live in the city and to enjoy being taught by leading scribes. It is understandable that his zeal now knew no bounds and that he became a fanatical opponent of all those who could not agree with his insights.

## The scandal of the cross

We cannot say with any certainty when Paul discovered that there were people living in Jerusalem who called themselves followers of Jesus of Nazareth. Luke relates that a young man called Saul was present at the stoning of Stephen (Acts 7.58) – the change of name from Saul to Paul only happened later (Acts 13.9). The author of the book of Acts also adds that Saul consented to the execution of Stephen (Acts 8.1). That need not surprise us, since as far as Paul was concerned Stephen belonged to a group within the early Christian community which was not afraid of criticizing certain commandments in the Torah with reference to Jesus (Acts 6.11–14). For a zealot of Paul's calibre the ideas of this group of followers of Jesus of Nazareth must have been a thorn in the flesh. As an expert in scripture he will not have found it difficult to refute their statements with a selection of quotations. In the light of scripture and tradition it seemed impossible to attach any positive significance to the death of a crucified man. The Old Testament does not yet know the word 'cross' in this significance. We do not know when the crucifixion of criminals, enemies and blasphemous opponents first took place among the Jews, but at all events it will not have been much earlier than around a century before the beginning of our era. Moreover it is not surprising that nowhere in the early Jewish tradition is there mention of the possibility that a *crucified* Messiah would bring salvation and redemption.

We can infer from one of his letters that Paul did find a text which in his view proved the contrary: 'cursed is anyone who hangs on the wood' (Gal. 3.13). With these words he is unequivocally referring to a passage from the Torah (Deut. 21.23). Of course Paul know that 'wood' in this text does not mean a cross, but a stake on which someone was stuck. However, this distinction will not have worried him very much. He had found a text which unmistakably showed that Jesus' disciples were wrong. In all probability it was because of his double background that he would not yield on this point. As a pious Jew he was opposed to belief in a crucified man, but his Graeco-Roman thought-world would also have led him to the same conclusion. Anyone who has been nailed to a cross is a failure: a runaway slave or a rebel has not succeeded in his aim. So it is folly to believe that salvation and redemption is to be expected from someone like that (I Cor. 1.23)!

The assertion of Jesus's followers that he had risen from the dead certainly would not have led Paul to think any differently. As a Pharisee, Paul believed in the resurrection of the dead. That event was seen as a decisive act in the final apocalyptic drama (Dan.12.1–3). While Paul was staying in Jerusalem there was no *shalom* in the country, but there could be no talk of an apocalyptic destruction of heaven and earth either. Moreover according to the apocalyptic expectation of the future, one man would not rise from the dead, but *all* human beings. So Paul had plenty of scriptural arguments to oppose to the claims of the followers of Jesus of Nazareth.

## Paul's 'conversion'

A good deal could be said about the surprising event near Damascus, but I shall restrain myself. I shall not go into the historical problems, because they may not be thought vital to our topic. But that certainly cannot be said of the consequences that this event had for Paul's life and thought. The Acts of the Apostles contains no less than three descriptions of Paul's experiences near Damascus. After first relating the story at length (Acts 9.1–19), Luke makes Paul give an account of the event near Damascus twice more (Acts 22.3–16; 26.9–18). Remarkably enough, in his own letters the apostle does not devote much attention to what was such an important event in his life. In his letter to the community of the Galatians he twice describes it as a 'revelation' (Gal. 1.12,16). From his choice of words we can infer that he found it an apocalyptic experience. Suddenly a light dawned on him and he discovered that the crucified Jesus had been raised by God from the dead.

For Paul, the consequences of this apocalyptic experience were so perplexing that he never succeeded in bringing any systematic order into the chaos of his conclusions and thoughts. As I have remarked, in the letter to the Galatians he describes the event as a 'revelation'. In his letter to the community in Philippi he uses terms which one could rightly call crass or even gross. After sketching out his zeal for the Jewish tradition in unequivocal terms, he goes on:

> But whatever gain I had, I counted as loss for the sake of Christ. Indeed I count everything as loss because of the surpassing worth of knowing Christ Jesus my Lord. For his sake I have suffered the loss of all things and count them as refuse, in order that I may gain Christ and be found in him, not having a righteousness of my own, based on law, but that which is through faith in Christ, the righteousness from God that depends on faith (Phil. 3.8–9).

Paul does not mince words. Did he ultimately interpret the 'revelation' that he was given on the way to Damascus as 'conversion'? And did he draw from this the conclusion that he had to break radically with the Jewish tradition? On the basis of the above passage from his letter to the community of Philippi, one would be all too inclined to answer these questions in the affirmative. That is all the more natural when we realize that the Greek word which the Revised Standard Version translates in a fairly neutral, inoffensive way needs to sound much more negative: filth, dung, or worse. Anyone who describes his past in such a way indubitably gives the impression of dissociating himself from it as radically as possible. Paul has been 'converted'; he has gone over from Judaism to the Christian community. And this is the way in which theologians and the church have preferred to interpret the event at Damascus down the centuries. Great theologians like Augustine and Luther even saw Paul's conversion as a model for their own conversions. They too realized at a particular moment, like a thunderbolt from a clear sky, that for a long time they had been going along the wrong path. They thought that they could share in God's grace through 'their own righteousness' – through their own good works and their own efforts. In the footsteps of the apostle Paul, as a result of their conversion they came to realize that they were completely dependent on God's grace and that one could only speak of reconciliation between God and human beings through the death of Christ on the cross. Were Augustine and Luther right to refer to Paul? The answer to this question must necessarily be complicated. To begin with, we need to be clear precisely what, in Paul's view, the content of this 'revelation' near Damascus was.

## An apocalyptic experience

Earlier I pointed out that Paul had had an apocalyptic 'revelation' near Damascus. What does that mean? For an answer to this question we need to look briefly at the Jewish apocalyptic view of the future and the world as it developed around the beginning of our era.

Unlike the majority of prophets in the Old Testament the apocalyptists, made wise by their troubles, arrived at the insight that *this* world is irredeemably lost. It no longer makes sense to hope for or to devote oneself to change and renewal. Evil has manifested itself world-wide to such a degree that the pious no longer need to pray for restoration, but for downfall and destruction. Apocalyptists write this world off completely. Renewal is possible only when the old has been broken up and destroyed. Then evil will be punished by God. As judge he will make his judgment on human actions. At first sight apocalyptic writings seem to contain only accounts of destruction. However, that is not the case. The pious have fixed their hope on God's faithfulness. God has a *new* world in mind, but only for the righteous, a world which is not made by human hands but which will descend from heaven as a gift from God. The apocalyptists know of the judgment that will take place: of course they fear it, but they do not despair: their faithfulness will be rewarded by God.

On his way to Damascus Paul received an apocalyptic vision. The surprising encounter with the crucified man whom God seemed to have raised from the dead changed his thinking totally. From this 'experience' he drew the conclusion that the resurrection of the dead – which is of essential importance in the apocalyptic view of the future – had become reality in principle. The fact that 'only' one dead man has been raised is suddenly no longer an obstacle for Paul. He now regards this as the beginning of the end, a hopeful sign: 'Christ as the firstfruits of those who sleep' (I Cor. 15.20). Christ has so to speak paved the way for the future.

Apocalyptists had quite a complicated notion of how things would go in 'the last days'. A popular thought was that the future would consist of two periods. The first phase would still take place totally on this earth. For several hundred years – there is no unanimity in early Jewish literature about the number: four hundred or seven thousand, but also two thousand or a thousand (cf. Rev. 20.1–6) – the righteous will prevail and *shalom* will rule. It is not unusual to describe this period as the 'messianic kingdom', and sometimes there is also mention of a messianic figure who functions as a symbolic figure. The first period will be concluded by the destruction of heaven and earth. After that the kingdom of God begins. The length of this period can no longer be expressed in figures: it will be eternal. For Paul this view of the future was important. That is clear especially from a complicated part of the first letter to the community in Corinth in which he writes about the role of Christ in the future: 'when he (= Jesus Christ) hands over the kingdom to God the Father' (I Cor. 15.24). Some verses later Paul adds: 'when all things are subjected to him (= God), the Son will also subject himself to him . . . that God may be all in all' (I Cor. 15.28).

Paul's expectation of the future with its apocalyptic colouring also gives us an answer to the question why Paul had such an obvious preference for the term 'Christ'. It is possible that he did not know that Jesus usually distanced himself from this title which, because of its 'royal' pretensions, could all too easily give rise to undesirable associations and arouse the wrong kind of expectations. But even if Paul was unaware of this, his preference still remains remarkable. As a scribe he must have known that there are no indications in scripture and tradition of a suffering Messiah, let alone a crucified Messiah. That Paul nevertheless has an unmistakable preference for the title Christ suggests that he quite deliberately gave it new content. For Paul, that Jesus is the Christ is connected above all with his apocalyptic experience at Damascus. At that time he discovered that the messianic kingdom had begun in principle, through the crucified Jesus who was raised from the dead by God. For Paul, that meant that Jesus of Nazareth must be the Christ.

Going further along that line, Paul arrives at the remarkable insight that he has already taken a step beyond the frontier between future and present: he no longer lives exclusively in *this* world but also already in the new world that is coming (Gal. 2.19–20; Rom. 6.1–14). The boundaries between present and future begin to be blurred. That brings the apostle to the audacious thought that in principle he has already left death behind – as a punishment for sins – and has become a new person. *Judgment*, too, belongs to the past. Paul need no longer worry about God's judgment. He is already justified, acquitted in a case without being required to present his defence. That is grace *par excellence*. Paul experiences liberation from sin, through Jesus Christ, or better, through the death of Jesus

Christ on the cross. What the apostle initially saw as a 'curse' proves to be a 'blessing' (Gal. 3.6–14).

## The crucified Christ at the centre

Paul's theological view bears the stamp of his apocalyptic experience. That he had learned to speak positively about the crucified man on the cross is the direct consequence of his encounter with the risen Lord. Without the raising of Jesus by God the cross would have remained a curse for him.

In church history and the history of dogma Paul's thought is often described as a *theologia crucis*, a theology of the cross, in other words a theology in which the crucified Christ has a central, 'crucial' role. Certainly such a characterization does not do Paul an injustice. But it is important not to lose sight of the direction of his thought. He did not become a disciple of Jesus Christ because he had been deeply impressed by his suffering and death on the cross. Paul had not been present then, and even if he had been, the sight would hardly have moved him very much. In the first place he would have found a crucified man repugnant and offensive. In the light of both his Jewish and his Graeco-Roman background he knew all too well that Jesus had died a shameful and humiliating death: 'We preach Christ crucified, a stumbling block to Jews and folly to Gentiles' (I Cor. 1.23). If we nevertheless want to describe Paul's view as *theologia crucis*, then we shall always need to remember that near Damascus he had learned a different way of thinking about the crucified Jesus. From that moment on he looks at the 'scandal' of the cross with eyes which have seen the light. In his letters Paul puts much emphasis on the cross and on the crucified Jesus (I Cor. 1.23; 2.2), but he pays virtually no attention to the 'narrative', the series of dramatic events which took place in Jerusalem years earlier. Paul was not very bothered about historical details, but concentrated on the theological significance of the death of Jesus Christ on the cross. Paul was a controversial figure. Passages in his letters indicated that he had to defend his apostleship against attack (Gal. 1.1; II Cor. 10–12). He had not been an eyewitness of Jesus' words and actions. He could not speak about the drama which took place in Holy Week on the basis of his own experience. Is that the reason why he is so strikingly silent about events from the life of Jesus? Did he not know enough and therefore thought it better to keep silent altogether? Did he make a virtue out of necessity? He is not (or no longer) interested in the past, because in the light of the cross and resurrection it seems no longer to be theologically relevant (II Cor. 5.16).

## The blessing of the cross

Paul wrote letters and not dogmatic studies. He was a practical man and not a scholar closeted in his study. He reacted to topical questions and tried to find simple solutions to problems which had arisen in communities which he had founded or which he still hope to visit – like the community of Rome. His view of the significance of the death of Christ on the cross cannot be easily expressed in a brief formula. In reaction to questions, Paul used a variety of images and notions, depending on the circumstances.

Anyone who wants to understand Paul needs primarily also to note his negative view of the cross. Terms like 'curse', 'folly' and 'scandal' fit into this framework. The question arises whether this negative aspect of the cross needs to be seen as a fate. Was Jesus the victim of evil – an unwilling victim? In the letter to the Galatians, as an introduction to the passage about 'the curse', there is a sentence which points in another direction: 'Christ redeemed us from the curse of the law, having become a curse for us . . .' (Gal. 3.13). Manifestly Jesus did not submit to this fate passively, but actively took it upon himself. Paul did not need to do any pioneer work in this area, but could take up notions which had already played an important role at an early stage in the young Christian community. That is evident from the tradition which he has used in his letter to the community of

Philippi (Phil. 2.6–11). The Lord quite deliberately chose the way that he took, a way of humiliation and sacrifice. Evil did not overwhelm him, but he accepted it.

Thus in the last instance the abhorrent sign of the cross even takes on a positive significance in Paul. It becomes the symbol of God's faithfulness and love of human beings. For Paul, a close connection develops between the symbol of the cross and the word 'grace'. As an expert on scripture and tradition the apostle will have had little difficulty in finding the relevant passages. I think it very probable that in so doing he also thought of the well-known sentences in Psalm 103: 'The Lord is merciful and gracious, slow to anger and abounding in steadfast love. He will not always chide, nor will he keep his anger for ever' (Ps. 103.8–9). I already quoted these words in an earlier chapter, but to my mind they are of such central importance for the biblical picture of God that I think it worth while quoting them explicitly once again here.

## Reflections on soteriology

I have already said often that Paul wrote letters and not dogmatic treatises; I shall say this once again to avoid any misunderstanding. Paul was a practical man and not a theoretician: he reacted to questions which were put to him and was not a systematic thinker. His letters do not enable us to penetrate the whole of his theological view and describe it in detail. Perhaps we still do him most justice if we conclude that his theology is 'incomplete'. The building is still in scaffolding, and it is even possible that the architect would want to demolish certain parts on closer inspection because they no longer fit into the whole or have no function in it.

All this is by way of introduction to this section, in which I shall begin to describe Paul's thoughts on 'soteriology': the significance of the suffering and death of Jesus on the cross. Anyone who sets out to investigate this immediately comes up against the problem that Paul wrote *letters*. His terminology is very diverse. Moreover he had a powerful imagination and made use of a surprising variety of images and notions. That, too, is a point which calls for the attention of readers. The language of the Bible is rich in metaphors. It cannot be otherwise, since it is impossible to speak of God and his Spirit, of creation and the future, of human ideas and religious experiences, other than metaphorically.

In the Bible God is usually referred to as 'he'. That, too, is an image, for God is beyond doubt more than a 'he' or a 'she'. God is given the title 'king' to express his power and glory. Well-known metaphors like 'father' and 'shepherd' illuminate yet other facets of God: he cares for his people as a father cares for his children. And like a shepherd who guides his sheep and protects them against wild animals, so God looks after those who walk in his ways. This can be made clear by metaphors in a way which language cannot achieve. It will prove that Paul also makes much use of metaphors in order to express aspects of soteriology. Metaphors are like pictures: they give a sketch, an impression of reality, but they cannot be identified with this reality. God is not a king but is *like* a king; he is not enthroned in a palace on earth, but use can be made of the metaphor of 'king' to say something about God.

If we compare the letters of Paul with one another we soon get the impression that the images come tumbling out headlong. I shall take as a starting point his letter to the Galatians – in my view it can be argued that this is the oldest writing in the New Testament. There is an interesting soteriological passage at the beginning of the epistle:

. . . the Lord Jesus Christ, who gave himself for our sins to deliver us from the present evil world (Gal. 1.3–4).

With these last words Paul makes no secret of the fact that his thought has been formed by the thought-world of apocalyptic. The purpose of the death of Jesus is – among other things – to deliver those who believe in him from the present evil age. In his first letter to the community of Thessalonica the apostle expresses ideas which are to some degree comparable (I Thess. 4.15–17). For Paul, this world no longer has any attraction and he even wishes that he could leave it. That will happen in any case at 'the coming of the Lord' (I Thess. 4.15), but in his letter to the community of Philippi he makes no secret of his longing to go 'to be with Christ, for that is far better' (Phil. 1.23). Some lines earlier he writes a sentence the clarity of which leaves little to be desired: 'For me to live is Christ and to die is gain' (Phil. 1.21).

Once again Paul indicates that he is not a systematic thinker. His encounter with the risen Lord has intensified his apocalyptic view of this world. He wants to be 'with Christ' and therefore he even longs to die. In the letter to the Galatians he uses yet another picture which is difficult to harmonize with those indicated above:

> For I through the law died to the law, that I might live to God. I have been crucified with Christ; it is not longer I that live, but Christ who lives in me (Gal. 2.19–20).

In his letter to the community in Rome, written later, he develops the notion further:

> Do you not know that all of us who have been baptized into Christ Jesus were baptized into his death? We were buried therefore with him by baptism into death, so that as Christ was raised from the dead by the glory of the Father, we too might walk in newness of life' (Rom. 6.3–4).

There is no mention in these texts of a longing for death. Nor is there any reason for that. Paul gives the impression that he is convinced that in fact he already has death behind him. In and with Christ's suffering and death, he himself has died and been buried, and then has been raised from the dead by God. His life on earth has become a new creation. Paul lives in two worlds.

The old and the new run side by side. Through Jesus Christ, the future has already become a reality. The present, earthly reality has taken on a totally different 'face' for those who believe. Those who know that death is finished for good as a punishment for sin can joyfully make an old prophetic expression their own: 'Death, where is your victory? Death, where is your sting?' (I Cor. 15.55; cf. Hos. 13.14). Paul puts the rhetorical question frankly and even triumphantly because the answer no longer causes him any anxiety.

## Died for us

After his overwhelming Damascus experience Paul knows that the death of Jesus on the cross has a paradoxical character. It is curse and blessing, folly and wisdom, defeat and victory both at the same time; the martyr death of one man proves to be a source of life for others. Paul will not have had much difficulty in adopting the notion that Christ died 'for us'. He did not need to do any pioneer work in this area, since, as we have already seen, this notion is a consequence of the Old Testament–Jewish tradition about the suffering of the innocent righteous. Paul knew scripture and he will have read with approval the relevant passages in the book of Psalms and the chapter about the suffering servant of the Lord in Isaiah 53.

In the first instance Paul takes up notions which were already known in the early Christian community. That is evident, for example, from a couple of texts in his first letter to the community of Corinth. Both times he begins with an introduction which reveals that he is largely dependent on tradition. In the first passage he describes the institution of the eucharist:

> For I received from the Lord what I also delivered to you, that the Lord Jesus on the night when he was betrayed took bread, and when he had given thanks, he broke it, and said, 'This is my body which is for you. Do this in remembrance of me.' In the same way also the cup, after supper, saying, 'This cup is

the new covenant in my blood. Do this, as often as you drink it, in remembrance of me.' For as often as you eat this bread and drink this cup, you proclaim the Lord's death until he comes (I Cor. 11.23–26).

The second passage forms the introduction to a long reflection on the reality and significance of the resurrection of Christ:

For I delivered to you as of first importance what I also received, that Christ died for our sins in accordance with the scriptures, that he was buried, that he was raised on the third day according to the scriptures (I Cor. 15.3–4).

Christ died on the cross 'for us' and he died 'for our sins'. This last notion is also not completely unknown in the Old Testament – although honesty compels to recognize that it is not in the foreground there. The Second Isaiah wrote an impressive piece about the suffering of the Servant of the Lord in which the following passages deserve special attention:

Surely he has borne our griefs and carried our sorrows; yet we esteemed him stricken, smitten by God, and afflicted.

But he was wounded for our transgressions, he was bruised for our iniquities; upon him was the chastisement that made us whole, and with his stripes we are healed . . . .

When he makes himself an offering for sin, he shall see his offspring, he shall prolong his days; by his knowledge shall the righteous one, my servant, make many to be accounted righteous; and he shall bear their iniquities.

Therefore I will divide him a portion with the great, and he shall divide the spoil with the strong; because he poured out his soul to death, and was numbered with the transgressors; yet he bore the sin of many, and made intercession for the transgressors (Isa. 53.4–6, 11–12).

Paul leaves no doubt that he knew this text. In his letter to the

community of Rome he unmistakably refers to it: 'Jesus our
Lord, who was put to death for our trespasses and raised for
our justification' (Rom. 4.24–25). The apostle's argument is not
so complicated at this point that it must remain obscure to us.
The death and resurrection of Christ form the key to understanding it. Those who are admitted into the messianic kingdom
have the judgment of God behind them and may know that they
are righteous, and pardoned by God; their sins are forgiven and
they are acquitted and liberated from guilt for good. Moreover
the prophet Isaiah already knew that God's grace knows no
limits: 'Though your sins are like scarlet, they shall be as white
as snow; though they are red like crimson they shall become like
wool' (Isa. 1.18).

It is understandable – I almost used the word 'logical' – that
Paul should make a connection between the cross and God's
judgment, and that he can therefore go on to speak of Jesus'
death as a death-for-us and even as a death-for-our-sins. Paul
need no longer experience the judgment; Christ did that 'for
him' on the cross. So the expression 'for us' or 'for him' can also
take on the meaning 'in our/his/my place'. That this notion was
not alien to Paul emerges from a text in the letter to the
Galatians: 'Christ redeemed us from the curse of the law,
having become a curse for us' (Gal. 3.13). The apostle conjures
up the picture of a slave market, a picture that was all too
familiar to the readers of the letter. That he was indeed thinking of the slave market can be inferred from the fact that later
in the letter he uses metaphors connected with slavery and freedom to clarify his standpoint (Gal. 4.1–7, 21–31). Christ has
made us free (Gal. 5.1) because he has ransomed us. Paul may
rightly be called the apostle of freedom.

## Bought and paid for

Metaphor have their limitations. They can be used to clarify
aspects of faith which cannot be made sufficiently clear with
ordinary words. Metaphors are simply aids. They are intended

as comparisons with reality and not as descriptions of reality. By way of clarification, here is just one instance. Any reader of the Fourth Gospel will understand, consciously or unconsciously, that John the Baptist is using a metaphor when he points to Jesus and says, 'Behold, the lamb of God, that takes away the sin of the world' (John 1.29). No one will imagine that a lamb was actually standing there.

I write this warning because church history and the history of dogma have taught us that metaphors can easily be misunderstood and even misused. In his letter to the Galatians Paul evokes the image of the slave market. In so doing he seeks to clarify an essential element of the death of Christ on the cross; he died for us and in our place; by this 'exchange' slaves are freed so that they gain 'the right of sons' (Gal. 4.6). With all these words and concepts the apostle still finds himself within the bounds of metaphor. It is also within this framework that the sentence 'Christ has redeemed us' (Gal. 3.13) needs to be interpreted. Such a comment is needed in order as it were to get the metaphor moving.

Readers go beyond the bounds of the metaphor if they ask to whom the ransom money is really paid. Paul does not go more closely into the question in this connection. With an eye to the conflict in Galatia he directs his attention first of all to the aspects described above. Yet there is a great temptation to extend the metaphor, all the more so because Paul himself prompts us to do so. In his first letter to the community of Corinth he uses a striking phrase twice in close succession, 'you were bought and paid for' (I Cor. 6.20; 7.22). These words, too, need to be understood as a metaphor. They function in a context in which freedom and slavery are similarly mentioned. It very much looks as if Paul remembered the metaphor in the letter to Galatians when he said this. He also wants to make it clear to the members of the community in Corinth that they have been liberated in Christ. Just as slaves were sometimes redeemed on the slave market by someone who was well disposed towards them, so now the same thing has happened to the community of Corinth: 'You have been bought and paid for.'

Paul has made the metaphor of the slave market so compact that there is a danger that misunderstandings may arise. Again there is a great temptation to extend the metaphor: to whom did the price for the freedom of the slaves have to be paid? Paul does not go into this question further. At this point he does not draw the consequences drawn by later generations. Once more it seems that Paul was not a systematic theologian, and perhaps we should also note that he knew better than to strive for a closed system. But where Paul's theology seemed incomplete, theologians in subsequent centuries sought to develop it systematically. In so doing they did not have enough of an eye for Paul's metaphorical language. He was using an image, not describing reality. Christ died for us and for our sins; he redeemed us from the slavery of sin and guilt; and the price he had to pay for that was his death on the cross. Paul does not say that the death of Jesus was a 'payment' to God which assuaged God's wrath. In my view, those who go that far in their interpretation are asking too much of the metaphor.

## Reconciliation

Paul constantly surprises us with his sense of reality. In his letters he tries to write as though he were standing next to people, and therefore he uses images and examples drawn from everyday life. Of course there is always the danger that nevertheless he will not be understood, or that his readers will run away with his metaphors. But anyone who constantly worries whether his words might be misunderstood or misused never puts pen to paper. The apostle to the Gentiles was certainly not that sort of person. No one who has read his letters would think of calling him timid. Of course it was daring to use the metaphor of the slave market to clarify the meaning of Jesus' suffering and death. Perhaps he offended some people by doing so, but the advantage was that he clarified an extremely difficult subject by means of an image which anyone could understand.

Paul is no less concrete when he introduces the term 'reconciliation' in the second letter to the community of Corinth. The text is complicated and needs to be discussed in detail. As we have already seen earlier, the starting point is Paul's typical notion that present and future have been put in a different perspective through the death and resurrection of Christ. The most important consequences of this fundamental reorientation include the conviction that those who believe in Christ encounter a new way of living. This time the apostle expresses his view like this:

Therefore, if any one is in Christ, there is a new creation; the old has passed away, behold the new has come (II Cor. 5.17).

Time and again it emerges that Paul took a great deal of trouble to explain precisely what it means for a believer to have become 'a new creation'. Among other things, here he makes use of terms like 'freedom' and 'justification'. He assures his readers that 'in Christ' they may live in a new relationship to God. If the cross is the place of God's judgment and the resurrection of the crucified Jesus provides proof of God's unconditional faithfulness and love, then it becomes evident that it is necessary to see the hand of God in all Jesus' life and death. God has taken the initiative in Christ by venturing to build a bridge to human beings who are alienated from him and who even live in enmity with him. Paul expresses this conviction in the following passage from the second letter to the Corinthians:

All this is from God, who through Christ reconciled us to himself and gave us the ministry of reconciliation; that is, in Christ God was reconciling the world with himself, not counting their trespasses against them, and entrusting to us the message of reconciliation.

So we are ambassadors for Christ, God making his appeal

through us. We beseech you on behalf of Christ, be reconciled to God. For our sake he made him to be sin who knew no sin, so that in him we might become the righteousness of God (II Cor. 5.18–21).

Dogmatic theologians regard this passage as one of the most important scriptural 'proof-texts' for the classical doctrine of the atonement. All the ingredients seem to be present: the divine initiative; the central role which Christ has played in all this; the 'exchange' which has taken place; and finally, as a negative apotheosis, the impossibility for human beings to redeem themselves by their own strength. Is the death of Jesus Christ indeed the sacrifice that must be offered to reconcile God with human beings?

Any discussion about reconciliation or atonement shows that it is very important to make a precise distinction between the different concepts and notions. In the passage quoted above, Paul uses Greek words which we translate as 'reconcile' and 'reconciliation'. But that does not mean that he wants to draw the attention of his readers to the sacrificial cult in the Jerusalem temple generally, or to the ritual of the Day of Atonement in particular. It is quite conceivable that he even tried deliberately to avoid this. We have come to know Paul as a practical and realistic person. He is writing the text about 'reconciliation' in a letter to the Christian community in Corinth, a Greek port and an important centre of trade and industry; a cosmopolitan city inhabited by people from every corner of the globe; a city with a temple, and also with brothels. It is evident from Paul's two letters that the oppositions within the Christian community were extraordinarily great (I Cor. 1.10–17). Opinions differed over a host of things, like eating meat offered to idols (I Cor. 8.1–13) and also visiting brothels (I Cor. 6.12–20). We can rightly speak of a very mixed community, Paul makes the utmost efforts to encourage growth towards unity (I Cor. 12–14).

The passage about reconciliation quoted above needs to be

put in this context. Paul makes no use of sacrificial terminology, and one can only be amazed at his wisdom. In the Christian community in Corinth, by doing this he could well have created more misunderstandings than solved problems. He would have to make it clear to his readers what differences there were between the sacrifices offered in Greek temples and the sacrificial rituals in the Jerusalem temple.

The Greek words which Paul has chosen derive from his 'ordinary' social dealings; in particular they played a role in the legal world. The apostle uses an image which is easy to follow. Two parties, two individuals or two groups, are at odds with each other. They have a conflict about something or other. It is easy to imagine the issue: a disagreement over a financial matter; a dispute over a legacy; a difference of opinion over a claim for damages. The question seems insoluble. Neither party will give way and the opposition is implacable. In such a situation someone is needed – a judge or an arbiter – to bring about reconciliation.

Paul uses this metaphor, derived from everyday daily life, to illuminate a facet of the consequences of Christ's suffering and death. God took the initiative in bridging the gulf and doing away with the enmity. Thanks to Christ, God and human beings can again live in peace with one another. Once again it is evident that too much must not be asked of the metaphor. The comparison works only partially. Whereas in human dealings parties usually remain irreconcilable, and an arbiter has to be introduced, in Paul's view one of the parties, God, takes the initiative in Christ to abolish the alienation. Certainly Christ functions as the intermediary between the two parties, but he does so at God's behest.

### 'Our Passover lamb has been slain'

Jesus was no Paul, and Paul was no Jesus. The differences between the two are great. But there are also agreements. Neither of them went around with his head in the clouds; they were both aware of those around them and their anxieties, and of ordinary everyday life. When Jesus spoke of the coming kingdom of God, he tried to make things clear by using comparisons from everyday life. He drew the attention of his audience to the farmer who sows and reaps; to the seed which grows and sometimes produces a surprising yield; to the behaviour of rich men, great landowners, landlords, merchants and traders. Sometimes Jesus' stories were touching: a woman loses a precious pearl; a shepherd goes in search of a lost sheep; a penitent son returns to his parents' home and is welcomed with open arms. Paul also uses comparisons from everyday life to clarify his viewpoints. From the images he uses it is evident that he has seen more of the world than Jesus. He travels a good deal outside Jewish territory and knows the Graeco-Roman cities with their slave markets and their law courts.

Paul and Jesus both visited the Jerusalem temple. As experts in scripture and tradition they will have been familiar with the rituals. But it is difficult to form a picture of their attitude towards the cult in Jerusalem. In accordance with the commandments of the Torah, Jesus 'went up to Jerusalem' as a pilgrim (Mark 10.32), one or several times, depending on the Gospel. On his arrival there he provoked fierce opposition on the part of the Jewish leaders because by analogy with the Old Testament prophets he emerged as a sharp critic of the way things were done in the temple (Mark 11.15–19; John 2.13–25). Otherwise there are hardly any other indications in the Gospels which can help us further in forming a judgment on Jesus' view of the sacrificial cult in the temple.

The evangelists prove to be no less silent about the celebration of the religious feasts. Only the Passover is mentioned in the Synoptic Gospels (Mark 14.1). The Fourth Evangelist adds the feast of Tabernacles (John 7.2) and the feast of Rededication (= Hanukkah, John 10.22). Remarkably, the Gospels never refer to the Day of Atonement (Lev. 16.1–34). It was taken for granted in later Christian tradition that in some way or another there was a connection between the 'atoning' suffering and death of Jesus Christ and the ritual of the Day of Atonement, but the four evangelists do not make any connection.

The apostle Paul also prefers to choose his comparative material close to home, in everyday life. But there are exceptions to every rule. In his first letter to the community in Corinth Paul talks of Christ as 'our Passover lamb which has been slain' (I Cor. 5.7). He puts this statement in a context in which one would not expect it. In this part of his letter he is not engaged in a fundamental reflection on the Old Testament–Jewish background to christology. Only a few chapters later he will consider the celebration of the Lord's supper (I Cor. 11.17–34), but then he says nothing about 'Christ as the Passover lamb'. The context in which he does use these words contains a tirade against gross sins in the Corinthian community: fornication and even forms of incest occur (I Cor. 5.1). The apostle is quite frank about this:

Your boasting is not good (I Cor 5.6).

To reinforce his statement he makes a comparison with the effect of yeast:

Do you not know that a little leaven leavens the whole lump? Cleanse out the old leaven that you may be a new lump, as you really are unleavened (I Cor. 5.6–7).

By way of association, Paul moves from the comparison with the effect of the yeast to the Jewish custom of removing all the old leaven prior to the celebration of the Passover in order to be able to celebrate the festival of unleavened bread as well as possible (Ex. 12.14–16). Paul continues his argument with a new association:

For Christ, our paschal lamb, has been sacrificed.
Let us, therefore, celebrate the festival, not with the old leaven, the leaven of malice and evil, but with the unleavened bread of sincerity and truth (I Cor. 5.7–8).

By means of a 'christological detour' – Christ as Passover lamb – Paul has returned to his tirade against sexual abuses in the community of Corinth. The course of this argument may be said to be typical of Paul. His letters are not distinguished by their clear systematic treatment of the issues. The apostle often allows himself be seized by his emotions. He goes on detours, and by associations make unexpected connections; sometimes there are leaps of thought which are not always easy to follow. Thus the metaphor of Christ as 'the Passover lamb that is slain' does not occur any of his other letters. So why does he use this image in this context?

Paul is deeply concerned about what in his eyes is the chaotic life of some members of the Christian community in Corinth. He urges them to live 'cleanly', and in order to give his words force he makes a comparison with an effect of yeast. It is not surprising that he goes on to associate this image with the celebration of Passover. The next step in a series of associations is less obvious and may certainly be said to be surprising. Passover clearly makes Paul think of a comparison between Christ and the Passover lamb. Was he the first to make such a connection, or does he depend on images which were already commonplace in the early Christian community? For want of sufficient information it is difficult to give a satisfactory answer to this question. It is certain that nothing is said about this in the three Synoptic Gospels. During Jesus' last supper with his disciples – the Seder meal – there is no mention of 'the Passover lamb that is slain'. Attention is drawn to the breaking of the bread and the giving of the wine (Mark 14.22–25). According to the Fourth Gospel John the Baptist, pointing to Jesus, is said to have called him 'the lamb of God' (John 1.29, 36), but there is a dispute as to whether he meant the Passover lamb here.

Paul does not make things easy for his readers. That is especially true of people who are consciously or unconsciously influenced by an age-old stream of theological ideas, of confessional writings and dogmas, of hymns and liturgical formulae. Contrary to what is often supposed, the Passover lamb was not a sacrificial animal in the strict sense of the term. At noon on the day before the Seder meal, priests slaughtered many hundreds and perhaps thousands of Passover lambs in the temple. However, they were not then offered to God on the altars, but taken back into the circle of family and friends to be eaten at a meal.

When Paul mentions 'Christ our Passover lamb' in his letter to the community in Corinth, he does not mean to present Christ as a sacrificial animal in a metaphorical way. If we are to understand him properly, we need to put the image in the direct context of his tirade against sexual abuses. The Christian community needs to be 'clean' – metaphorically 'unleavened'. It can be so, because Jesus as 'the Passover lamb which has been slain' has led the way. In fact Paul is saying the same thing in other words and images when he writes that in Christ they are a new creation.

## The mercy seat

There is just one more statement of Paul's which needs to be investigated closely in this connection. In his letter to the community in Rome there is a particularly complicated passage which contains a reference to the temple cult in Jerusalem. The topic is the 'righteousness of God', and above all the way in which this 'has been made manifest' (Rom. 3.21). Paul argues that this has happened 'outside the law', namely 'through faith in Jesus Christ' (Rom. 3.22). The consequence is that this 'righteousness of God' is for 'believers', and no distinction is made any longer between Jews and Gentiles (Rom. 1.16–17).

Paul draws attention to the crucified Christ, as he also does in his other letters. We already noted earlier that Paul was a creative man, blessed with a rich imagination and with a many-sided cultural and religious background. In this passage his vocabulary is surprising, and he introduces a metaphor which he has in any case taken not from Graeco-Roman civilization, but from the Old Testament commandments and precepts.

Some exegetes are so impressed by the differences from the images and notions that Paul uses in his other letters that they have come to the conclusion that in this passage he is largely dependent on tradition. In other words, these are not his own words, but he has chosen formulations which had already been developed in the early Christian community – it is not very difficult to find examples which suggest that he often worked in such a way (e.g. I Cor. 15.3–4; Phil. 2.6–11).

> Since all have sinned and fall short of the glory of God, they are justified by his grace as a gift, through the redemption which is in Christ Jesus,
> *whom God put forward as an expiation by his blood, to be received by faith* (Rom. 3.23–25).

First of all, the translation of the words in italics poses the difficult problems. Paul uses a Greek term which in most translations is rendered 'means of expiation' or 'means of atonement'. That may indeed be correct, but such terms do not make sufficiently clear precisely what Paul was thinking of when he set down these words. The Greek term which raises so many questions appears only once in the New Testament: in the chapter in the letter to the Hebrews in which there is a description of the Old Testament 'tent of meeting'. In this context the translation of the Greek word used is not problematical: the mercy seat (Heb. 9.5). This rendering finds support in the Septuagint, the Greek translation of the Old Testament writings. In the book of Exodus there is a brief description of the mercy seat. It is on the ark and is framed by two cherubim:

> And you shall put into the ark the testimony which I shall give you.
> Then you shall make a mercy seat of pure gold; two cubits and a half shall be its length, and a cubit and a half its breadth.
> And you shall make two cherubim of gold; of hammered work shall you make them, on the ends of the mercy seat.

> Make one cherub on the one end, and one cherub on the other end; of one piece with the mercy seat shall you make the cherubim on its two ends.
>
> The cherubim shall spread out their wings above, overshadowing the mercy seat with their wings, their faces one to another; toward the mercy seat shall the faces of the cherubim be (Ex. 25.16–20).

The mercy seat plays a key role in the ritual for the Day of Atonement (Lev. 16.1–34). At the beginning of the description it is said that 'God will appear in the cloud above the mercy seat' (v.2). Then the high priest enters the sanctuary alone and there makes a number of sacrifices.

> And he shall take some of the blood of the bull, and sprinkle it with his finger on the front of the mercy seat, and before the mercy seat he shall sprinkle the blood with his finger seven times.
>
> Then he shall kill the goat of the sin offering which is for the people, and bring its blood within the veil, and do with its blood as he did with the blood of the bull, sprinkling it upon the mercy seat and before the mercy seat.
>
> Thus he shall make atonement for the holy place, because of the uncleannesses of the people of Israel, and because of their transgressions, all their sins; and so he shall do for the tent of meeting, which abides with them in the midst of their uncleannesses (Lev. 16.14–16).

These actions are performed by the high priest, since he is the only one in the sanctuary. After that he goes outside, to the altar 'which is before the Lord', and performs a comparable ritual with another part of the blood in the sight of the people (Lev. 16.18–19). All these actions by the high priest are described in the Torah as 'atoning for the holy place and the tent of meeting and the altar' (Lev. 16.20). By the sacrifices and the sprinkling of blood, 'holy places' which had been made unclean by the sins and injustices of the people are atoned for. Only when these rituals have been performed does the sending away of the 'scapegoat' take place:

> And Aaron shall lay both his hands upon the head of the live goat, and confess over him all the iniquities of the people of Israel, and all their transgressions, all their sins; and he shall put them upon the head of the goat, and send him away into the wilderness by the hand of a man who is in readiness.
>
> The goat shall bear all their iniquities upon him to a solitary land; and he shall let the goat go in the wilderness (Lev. 15.21–22).

The whole ritual is complicated and not clear in every respect. However, we can suppose that a distinction must be made between the specific functions of the various rituals. Animals are sacrificed and the sprinkling of the blood on the mercy seat symbolizes the atoning for the 'holy places'. In connection with that the transgressions of the people are removed from the community. That happens through two rituals which make the removal very tangible. First of all the high priest puts his hands on the goat's head and in so doing transfers the people's sins to the animal; then it is sent out into the wilderness. In this way the transgressions are removed from the midst of the community of the people of God and it is possible for it to begin with a clean sheet.

What was the apostle Paul thinking of when he included this passage in his letter to the Roman community? There is no doubt whatsoever that he will have known the ritual of the Day of Atonement. It may be clear that he is not primarily comparing Jesus with the scapegoat that is sent into the wilderness. From the fact that Paul deliberately uses the phrase 'in his blood', we must infer that he is primarily referring to the ritual which took place within the sanctuary. That would mean that he compared Christ with the mercy seat. It is understandable how there has been some hesitation about translating the passage in the letter to the Romans in this sense, since beyond question it is a strange comparison. But the metaphor is not impossible in Paul's argument. The crucified Christ is central to his view. We have already noted earlier that the cross has a paradoxical character in his thought: it is 'curse' and 'blessing'; it is the place of the judgment of God and at the same time, in combination with the raising of Christ by God, the beginning of the new creation; and thus also the place where the reconciliation between God and human beings takes place. In the ritual of the Day of Atonement it is understandable that this place should be compared with the mercy seat. The sprinkling of the blood on the mercy seat brings about atonement for the holy places. In this way the possibility is created of doing away with the sins of the people and a way is made for bringing about a new relationship with God.

At the end of this section something more seems to be said about the significance of 'the blood of Christ'. As is well known, this terminology has had great influence in church history and the history of dogma. Phrases like 'his precious blood' and 'the blood of Christ that cleanses us from our sins' are presumably all too well known to readers. In a later chapter I shall go into this facet of the atonement in more detail. As far as Paul is concerned, it can be concluded that in his letters he only used this terminology by way of exception, and very rarely (Rom. 3.25; 5.9; I Cor. 10.16; 11.25–27). Despite his knowledge of the Old Testament sacrificial cult he preferred to use metaphors and comparisons taken from everyday reality. He felt called into the Gentile world to proclaim the gospel of Jesus Christ. For that reason he chose his imagery with care and made sparse use of comparisons with the sacrificial cult in Jerusalem.

## Conclusion

It is no small task to do justice to a complicated thinker like Paul in a limited number of pages. He was an excitable and emotional man. He knew that he was a 'zealot' and did not conceal his pride in this (Gal. 1.14; 3.6). His experience near Damascus changed his life decisively. He wanted a great deal and wanted it all at the same time. He entered the Gentile world, but he was and remained a Jew and would never deny his Old Testament–Jewish background. In order to win over the Gentiles, in the letter to the Galatians he set the Torah aside, but he would have thought it senseless to do away with the Torah for good. Through scripture and the tradition he knew what grace was, but his encounter with the crucified and risen Lord deepened and radicalized his knowledge. At the same time he was not a man to sit still. He was convinced that 'Christ died for us', but he did not stop there. The way of Christ was also the way he needed to take to God, and he also repeatedly points to this way in his letters. Thus the splendid Christ hymn in the second chapter of his letter to the community in Philippi stands in the following framework.

Let this mind be in you which was also in Christ Jesus (Phil. 2.5).

Paul too had this 'mind'. It was his wish to be an active disciple of the crucified Jesus.

# 5

# After Paul

## On unknown territory

Paul wrote his letters over a period of almost ten years – from the end of the 40s to the end of the 50s of the first century of our era. They make it possible for us to form a picture of the first decades of church history. However, exegetes need to be careful about drawing conclusions and modest in defending viewpoints. The sources at our disposal are only a few letters addressed to a limited number of Christian communities spread over a large area, from the middle of Asia Minor via Greece to the city of Rome. Our knowledge of the past is therefore very fragmentary. We might compare it to an incomplete jigsaw puzzle: over the course of the years many of the pieces have been lost.

The Acts of the Apostles fills only a few gaps. Luke wrote this sequel to his Gospel probably not earlier than the 80s. Moreover a close comparison between the letters of Paul and the book of Acts shows that they do not always shed the same light on the past. That is especially true of Paul's activity after his Damascus experience. In his letter to the Galatians the apostle himself emphasizes that he did not go to Jerusalem immediately afterwards, but travelled to Arabia. Only three years later did he go to Jerusalem for a visit to Peter which lasted fifteen days (Gal. 1.17–19). By contrast Luke relates that Paul travelled to Jerusalem immediately after his adventurous departure from Damascus (Acts 9.23–26). Whether either of the two offers a historically reliable account cannot be demonstrated beyond question. In the first instance the tendency is to put great trust in what Paul says. He himself was there and therefore he would know best what happened. But he too has 'interests' when he describes the past. Above all in his letter to the Galatians he does all he can to demonstrate his independence of the brothers in Jerusalem. God and no one else chose him and called him to be an apostle of Jesus Christ (Gal. 1.14–17). Of course Luke too had to defend 'interests'. He attached great importance to the unity of the early Christian community. He felt that it was important to show that Paul had gone to Jerusalem as quickly as possible after his 'conversion' near Damascus in order to make contact there with the apostles who had formerly been disciples of Jesus.

Paul wrote letters and that was certainly no luxury, since there were many pressing questions in the early Christian communities and the divisions among them were great. Thus there was a disagreement in Galatia over the significance of the commandments of the Torah for Christians who had come from the pagan world. Had they to be circumcised, or did such commandments not apply to them? We can learn from the book of Acts that this problem was a source of anxiety in a number of other communities (Acts 15.1–34), but through Paul's letter we have by far the best information about the community in Galatia. In this letter the apostle gives a surprisingly 'scriptural' view on this question. He emphasizes the universal character of God's promise to Abraham – 'in you shall all peoples be blessed' (Gen. 12.3; Gal. 3.8). Paul concludes from the fact that this promise precedes the Torah both chronologically (Gal. 3.17) and qualitatively (Gal. 3.19–20) that Gentiles who enter the Christian community need not submit to the yoke of circumcision: they are justified by faith in Jesus Christ and not by works of the law (Gal. 2.16).

Much is required of Paul's theological imagination and creativity. His preaching about the 'coming of the Lord' (I Thess. 4.15) had made so much of an impact on the community of Thessalonica that problems arose when time passed and some of its members died. The letter to the community of

Philippi initially has a cheerful and excited tone and gives the impression that there are no problems, but the tone in the second part is different, and in this community, too, there seem to be differences about the significance of the Torah (Phil. 3.2–16). Life in the great cosmopolitan port of Corinth is so chaotic and there are so many deviations – from eating meat offered to idols to prostitution – that the Christian community risks going under for lack of guidance. Paul had great difficulty in gaining a hearing for his views. He wrote at least two letters, but there are indications that he sent more letters to Corinth (I Cor. 5.9; II Cor. 2.4; 7.8). It is quite uncertain whether all his efforts met with success. Paul's letters have been preserved for posterity, but we cannot say what effect they had. After so many centuries we have got used to their canonical status, but they did not yet have that status when they were read aloud in cities like Thessalonica, Philippi, Corinth and Rome. Perhaps they were sometimes accepted as authoritative, but it seems certain that they also provoked annoyance and opposition. Paul often spoke quite bluntly, and he was not always diplomatic (Gal. 3.1; 5.12). Even then, the motto was, 'People in glass houses don't throw stones.'

## Supporters

Paul had supporters and he also formed a 'school'. It is evident from his letters that he could draw on a wide circle of fellow-workers. In the initial phase of his activities, Barnabas was his firm companion (Acts 11.19–15.34). A serious dispute put an end to their collaboration (Acts 15.35–16.3). From then on Paul was associated with other men like Silas, Timothy and later also with Luke, Titus and others.

Letters have come down from these circles which bear the name of Paul but in all probability were not written or dictated personally by him, as was his custom (Rom. 16.22; Gal. 6.11). The letter to the community of Colossae is closest to the 'authentic' letters of Paul. The name of Timothy as the possible author crops up in scholarly literature from time to time – he is also mentioned in the introduction (Col. 1.1). His affinity with Paul is so great that this could explain the agreements; at the same time he is someone else and it is understandable that he should have chosen different words and terms. There is a considerable likeness between this letter and the letter to the Ephesians. It is generally assumed that an unknown author conceived the latter on the model of the letter to Colossae.

For our topic it is interesting that in the first chapter of the letter to the Colossians there is a passage which is very reminiscent of a hymn (1.15–23) and which involuntarily evokes memories of the well-known passage in Paul's letter to the community of Philippi (Phil. 2.6–11; cf. I Tim. 3.16). The author of the letter to Colossae has taken this hymn from the tradition and worked on it in the light of his christological insights. The formulation suggests that the original hymn comes from a Hellenistic–Jewish milieu – here we should think of the influential Jewish community of Alexandria in Egypt – in which speculations about the pre-existent wisdom of God were a popular theme (Prov. 8.22–30). The hymn in the letter to the community of Colossae must be read and interpreted against this specific background.

> He is the image of the invisible God, the first-born of all creation; for in him all things were created, in heaven and on earth, visible and invisible, whether thrones or dominions or principalities or authorities – all things were created through him and for him. He is before all things, and in him all things hold together (Col. 1.15–17).

Thus far the words fit the Hellenistic Jewish tradition completely. That changes in the following lines. Here I should point out that it proves extremely difficult to indicate the precise points at which the author of the letter has introduced alterations to the original hymn:

. . . and he is the head of the body, the church.

He is the beginning, the firstborn from the dead, that in everything he might be pre-eminent. For in him all the fullness of God was pleased to dwell, and through him to reconcile to himself all things, whether on earth or in heaven, making peace by the blood of his cross (Col. 1.18–20).

It will not have escaped attentive readers that these texts express thoughts which were not foreign to Paul. Here I am thinking in particular of the phrase 'the firstborn from the dead' (v.18). As we were able to note in the previous chapter, this view of things was of central importance to Paul. What is new is (a) the strong accent on the pre-existence of Christ – in Gal. 4.4 the sentence 'But when the fullness of time had come God sent his Son' seems almost to presuppose this pre-existence – and (b) the fact that Christ appears as 'collaborator' with the Creator at the creation.

It is important for our concern that the verb 'reconcile' also occurs in this hymn (v.20; cf. v.21, where the word is repeated). It is remarkable that the terminology in the letter to the community of Colossae is closely related to, but not completely like, the terms which Paul used in the passage about reconciliation in the second letter to the community in Corinth (II Cor. 5.17–21). No less striking is the phrase 'having made peace by the blood of his cross' (v.20). Both the 'having made peace' and 'the blood of his cross' are terms which we look for in vain elsewhere in the New Testament. There is no doubt that here we come into contact with notions which have been taken from Paul but which are expressed in a new and different way.

The anonymous author of the letter to the Ephesians goes further along this line. That is true both of the attention to the blood of Christ and the idea that the work of Christ can be summed up with the word 'peace'. Here, by way of illustration, are the relevant texts:

In him we have redemption through his blood, the forgive-

ness of our trespasses, according to the riches of his grace
(Eph. 1.7).
But now in Christ Jesus you who once were far off have been
brought near in the blood of Christ (Eph. 2.13).

The second text forms the introduction to a section in which the
author develops a view which we may think to be of central
importance to him. He does so with the help of thoughts taken
from Paul's 'authentic' letters and the letter to the community of
Colossae. The 'blood of Christ' brings about reconciliation not
only between God and human beings but also among human
beings and especially between Jews and Gentiles, between
circumcised and uncircumcised. So those 'who once were far off
have been brought near':

> For he is our peace, who has made us both one, and has
> broken down the dividing wall of hostility, by abolishing in
> his flesh the law of commandments and ordinances, that he
> might create in himself one new man in place of the two, so
> making peace, and might reconcile us both to God in one
> body through the cross, thereby bringing the hostility to an
> end (Eph. 2.14–16).

It very much seems that here in 'the school of Paul' not the last,
but certainly the loftiest and most profound, word about the
significance of the suffering and death of Jesus Christ is said.
In the Pastoral Epistles – the letters addressed to Timothy
(two of them) and Titus – new terms may be introduced, but
they unmistakably function within the framework of Paul's
theology:

> This is good, and it is acceptable in the sight of God our
> Saviour, who desires all men to be saved and to come to the
> knowledge of the truth. For there is one God, and there is one
> mediator between God and men, the man Christ Jesus, who
> gave himself as a ransom for all (I Tim. 2.3–5).

Time passes. The Christian church begins to become an institution. Leadership must be given. Rules and regulations are needed. The 'authentic' letters of Paul do not contain adequate instructions. Doubtless the unknown author of the Pastoral Epistles was providing for a need. The result was that he devoted more attention to how things were going in the community than to further christological reflection. He calls Christ a 'mediator' but also 'saviour' (II Tim. 1.10; Titus 1.4), although he can say that of God (I Tim. 1.1). However much this title may have become established for Jesus Christ in church history, it occurs only very sporadically in the four Gospels: in Luke's account of the birth of Jesus (Luke 2.11) and in the pericope in the Fourth Gospel about Jesus' encounter with the woman of Samaria (John 4.42). Clearly the notion of Christ as 'saviour of the world' developed only at a relatively late stage. Finally, the last sentence that I quoted above, 'the man Christ Jesus, who gave himself as a ransom for all', also shows a remarkable affinity with the Synoptic Gospels. It is not precisely the same term, but it agrees closely with an important sentence which is to be found in the Gospels of Matthew and Mark:

> For the Son of man also came not to be served but to serve, and to give his life as a ransom for many (Mark 10.45; Matt. 20.28).

## Opponents

Paul created a school, but he also provoked opposition. In the previous section I looked at the viewpoints of his supporters. It is far more difficult to get an idea of the views of his critics. We may take it as certain that there were some. The apostle was a passionate man, initially a zealot for the traditions of his ancestors (Gal. 1.14), and after his Damascus experience he was a no less fervent follower of Jesus Christ. He chooses standpoints which were certainly not undisputed and he adopts courses which must have led to conflicts.

Which of his views could have raised questions? Certainly his claim to be an apostle of Jesus Christ. That he was sharply attacked on this point is evident from passages in various letters (Gal. 1.11–24; II Cor. 11–13). With great fierceness and sometimes with razor-sharp irony (II Cor. 11.21–29), he refuses to give an inch and defends his apostleship vigorously.

He caused difficulties by the zeal with which he tried to introduce the gospel of Jesus Christ to the pagan world. It seems that his successes in the mission field outside the Jewish sphere were so great that theological reflection had so to speak to run to keep up with the facts. What place and function did the Torah still have? Paul made a choice, but his choice came up against the opposition of Jewish Christians who would not have any compromise over the significance of the Torah. On the other hand it is also quite conceivable that Paul's standpoint came up against difficulties among some Gentile Christians because they regarded him as too moderate, too Jewish. They would have preferred a radical break with the Jewish tradition and as a logical consequence of that the abolition of the Torah in the Christian community. Despite his careful relativizing of the significance of the Torah for Gentile Christians, Paul never went so far as to argue that God's commandments should no longer be obeyed. However, we must think that after his death – presumably in the middle of the 60s – above all in the communities in which pagan Christians were in a considerable majority, a tendency gradually developed radically to cut the theological 'knot' which the apostle had left behind, which was so difficult to untie.

It is quite possible that the letter of James should be read as a critical reaction to radical views of some of Paul's followers: faith without works is dead faith (James 2.14–26). The Sermon on the Mount in the Gospel of Matthew is also extremely critical of those who think that the commandments of the Torah no longer have any significance for the Christian community:

Think not that I have come to abolish the law and the

prophets; I have come not to abolish them but to fulfil them (Matt. 5.17).

Which of Paul's views would also have provoked criticism? As we know, he was remarkably one-sided in his view of Jesus Christ. Paying virtually no attention ot the life of Jesus, he puts all the emphasis on his suffering and death. The crucified Jesus and the cross occupy a central place and nothing else seems to be important. Is Paul making a virtue out of necessity? We may imagine that former disciples of Jesus accused him of this. They could tell attractive stories about Jesus' words and deeds. If Paul had had his way, these stories would have been forgotten. Fortunately that did not happen, and thanks to the efforts of the evangelists they have been preserved.

# 6

# The Synoptic Gospels

*Back to the past*

In retrospect it seems natural that Gospels should have been written in the early Christian community. But honesty compels us to recognize that this was less obvious than might perhaps seem at first sight. The letters of the apostle Paul indicate that the Christian community could grow rapidly without detailed recollections of the life of Jesus. What sense does it then make to turn one's attention to the past? Paul thought that there was no point in following this course (II Cor. 5.16). He believed that 'the time was short' (I Cor. 7.29). Living in the expectation of the speedy coming of the Lord, he did not think that it made sense to spend time dwelling on the past. The future beckoned and offered a hopeful perspective.

The fact that Gospels were nevertheless written indicates that Paul's views were not shared by everyone. Moreover time was passing. The Gospels were written between one and three decades after Paul's letters. These were turbulent years. A good deal happened, and there were far-reaching changes. The disciples of the first hour, the men and women who had been disciples and eye-witnesses, died one after another. How could memories of the past be preserved for posterity? In the middle of the 60s tension increased within Palestinian Judaism. Hostilities broke out everywhere and the success of the Maccabees seemed to be being repeated. The initial euphoria quickly ended in a terrible bloodbath. The Roman empire was more powerful than the armies of the Syrian king in 164 BC. The revolt was put down with a hard hand, the city of Jerusalem captured and the temple destroyed.

Those who might have thought that this was the end of the world expected by the apocalyptists soon found that they were wrong. Time went on as usual. The messianic kingdom seemed to be further away than ever. The Messiah, the son of David, did not come to restore order. Nothing special happened, and the pious realized very quickly that they would do better to stick to the Torah than to pursue attractive, seductive apocalyptic dreams which seemed to be deceptive. However, the disillusionment was not just limited to Jewish circles. In the meantime expectations had become tense in the early Christian community: the coming (or the return) of Christ could not be delayed much longer.

It was in this confusing, chaotic situation that the evangelists wrote their Gospels. What did they want to achieve? What was their concern? Were they historians and did they strive to clarify the past? Or did they hope as it were through the past to find illumination for the times in which they were living? In the course of history very different answers have been given to such questions. For centuries the view prevailed that the evangelists had to be seen as historically reliable chroniclers. They describe what had really happened. People still did not notice the countless differences between the Gospels or proved extremely creative and inventive in discovering solutions and harmonizations.

By means of historical criticism of the Bible, the scholarly view of the history of the composition of the Gospels has changed very considerably since the nineteenth century. Exegetes came to realize that the evangelists had been dependent on both oral and written traditions. The consequence was that the authority of the evangelists was considerably reduced. They were now said to have done no more than gather the tradition and put it in order. They were not thought capable of an independent view of the significance of the life and death of Jesus. Like all spheres of culture and science, so too theology has experienced its waves and changes of fashion. Shortly after the Second World War the conviction gained ground that the contribution of the evangelists to the process of the formation of the Gospels could no longer be trivialized. The writers of the Gospels did not deserve to be called simply 'collectors'. They had the right to be seen as the first generation of 'theologians': in their striving to actualize the past they selected and worked on the stories and sayings that they found in the tradition.

Fifty years later, we can conclude that the initial enthusiasm about the discovery of the theological achievements of the Gospels has now cooled once again. In the span of around half a century a flood of books and articles has appeared in which the 'theologies' of the individual evangelists have been analysed. Anyone who might have hoped that at long last something like a consensus might develop has to see that differences of opinion are now greater rather than less. At present caution seems called for. There is a danger that exegetes want to make the text say more than the writer ever intended.

## The tradition

This is not the place to go in detail into the question precisely what happened to the oral and written tradition between the life and death of Jesus on the one hand and the moment when the Gospels were written on the other. This is a period of between forty and sixty years. Little can be said with certainty about the theological developments in that period. I shall limit myself to the results of research which have found a degree of consensus and which might be thought important for the topic of this book.

The history of the origin of the three Synoptic Gospels is a complicated one. The majority of exegetes today take the hypothesis that Mark wrote the earliest Gospel as the starting point for their investigations. Matthew and Luke knew the Gospel of Mark or were familiar with the oral and written traditions which underlie it. Both evangelists took over and worked on the tradition, each in his own way – Matthew has far more in common with Mark than Luke has. In addition, the two evangelists had a second common source, which in scholarly literature has been given the name Q (for German *Quelle*, source).

Although nothing can be said for certain about the extent and form – oral or written – of the Q source, a scholarly consensus has developed about the theological profile of Q. In all probability the source contained mainly sayings of Jesus and few narratives, if any. Among other things that means that Q did not have a passion narrative. In the sayings which can probably be attributed to Q there are no explicit references to the suffering and death of Jesus. The picture of him which is evoked in this source can be briefly summed up as follows: Jesus is the apocalyptic prophet who lives in a tense expectation of the speedy coming of the Son of man. He admonishes his followers about this, calls on them to repent and commits them to living from now on in accordance with the commandments which will apply in this kingdom.

There is a striking agreement between the Q source and the non-canonical Gospel of Thomas which was discovered in Nag Hammadi in 1945. This formed part of a small library of Gnostic writings from the first centuries of Christianity. Whether the Gospel of Thomas must be regarded as a Gnostic work is a much-disputed question. The composition of this apocryphal Gospel is surprising. Like the Q source it consists of sayings – 114 in all – and contains no stories about Jesus' activity. Nor is any attention paid to the suffering and death of Jesus in these sayings. In sharp contrast to the letters of Paul, the cross and the crucified Jesus are not at all central in the Gospel of Thomas. Precisely how Gnostic it is need not concern us further here. It is certain that some sayings appear in it which could be old – dating perhaps even from the 50s of the first century. According to the Gospel of Thomas, Jesus was a teacher of alternative wisdom. The kingdom of God here is not a phenomenon of the future. It is already present and can be 'seen' by those who have arrived at deeper insight and wisdom through Jesus' words.

## Mark

Chronologically speaking, this shortest Gospel should come first. Mark has the honour of having been the first evangelist. However, there is a dispute about what individual the name conceals. In this book I shall not adopt any position in the scholarly debate, because it is not of fundamental importance for investigating the way in which the early Christian community reflected on the significance of the suffering and death of Jesus. That also applies to the other well-known classic introductory questions: when and for whom did the evangelist write?

It is clear that the author was not an eye-witness. In the early church he was called 'the interpreter of Peter'. The value of this information is doubtful. It is not inconceivable that in this way an attempt was made to give the Gospel of Mark more 'canonical' and above all 'apostolic' authority. The author may not himself have been an apostle, but he appeared as the spokesman of no less a figure than Peter. Moreover the tradition of the early church also makes a critical comment. Mark is said not always to have put Peter's stories in the right order.

What did Mark intend by writing his Gospel? Does he have a theological view of the past? Does he give any sign of having been intensely preoccupied with fundamental christological reflection? The danger is that as modern exegetes and readers we may easily ask too much of Mark. The evangelist was not a learned theologian by profession. His work was once described as 'primitive'. At first sight that perhaps does not sound very positive, but it is not impossible that it does most justice to the evangelist. With simple literary means and without too many words he goes directly to his goal: a very extensive account of the suffering and death of Jesus. However, in contrast to his 'haste' – a favourite word of Mark's is 'immediately' – he takes a strikingly long time to tell stories about the miracles which Jesus did.

During his baptism by John, Jesus discovers that he has been called by God in a special way, 'You are my Son' (Mark 1.11).

From that moment on he comes forward to proclaim the imminent coming of the kingdom of God (Mark 1.14–15), as a healer and exorcist. The one who after his baptism by John is endowed with the spirit of God comes into conflict with evil spirits which can take possession of people and be a real torment to them.

The earliest evangelist offers relatively few new perspectives on the suffering and death of Jesus. He seems to be largely dependent on the passion narrative which had already been put down in writing before him in the early Christian community of Jerusalem. As we already saw, in this account the events in the last week of Jesus' life in Jerusalem were put above all in the context of the Old Testament–Jewish tradition of the righteous sufferer. The evangelist Mark takes this up. A couple of texts emphasize that the suffering of Jesus can be described as 'a suffering for others':

> For the Son of man also came not to be served but to serve, and to give his life as a ransom for many (Mark 10.45).

The second text is part of the description of the words which Jesus spoke at the Seder meal, his last meal with his disciples:

> Take, this is my body
>
> . . .
>
> This is my blood of the covenant which is shed for many (Mark 14.22–25).

Both texts contain allusions to Isaiah 53, the impressive pericope about the suffering servant of the Lord, which is part of the tradition about the suffering of the righteous.

## Matthew

The author of the Gospel with the most chapters – we shall continue to call him Matthew for convenience, although here too it is not certain precisely who lies behind this name – confronts the exegete with a number of complicated questions. Half a century of intensive investigation of his 'theology' has not produced a satisfying result. There are too many voices in the Gospel which are not in harmony with one another. Matthew opens his Gospel with a genealogy in which we are left in no doubt of Jesus' Old Testament–Jewish origin: 'Jesus Christ, the son of David, the son of Abraham' (Matt. 1.1). Above all in the birth narrative, Matthew accompanies his description of events with a typical commentary: 'All this took place to fulfil what the Lord had spoken by the prophet' (Matt. 1.22; cf. 2.5, 15, 17, 23). More than any other evangelist, Matthew emphasizes that the whole of Jesus' life must be seen as a fulfilment of the prophetic expectations of the Old Testament. The logical consequence of this approach is that the appearance of Jesus remains within the limits of the Jewish tradition. Moreover it is in this sense that Jesus reacts to the urgent request of a Canaanite woman for him to heal her daughter: 'I am sent only to the lost sheep of the house of Israel' (Matt. 15.24). Some chapters earlier Jesus had sent his disciples out with more or less the same words: 'Go nowhere among the Gentiles, and enter no town of the Samaritans, but go rather to the lost sheep of the house of Israel' (Matt. 10.5–6). At the end of the Gospel Jesus' followers are given a completely different command: 'Go and make disciples of all nations' (Matt. 28.19). From what perspective should the Gospel be read – from the universalist conclusion or from the particularized beginning?

According to Matthew, Jesus emphasized the abiding significance of the Torah in his Sermon on the Mount in unmistakable words (Matt. 5.17). Moreover he also expects this disciples to be 'super-Pharisees': 'For I tell you, unless your righteousness exceeds that of the scribes and Pharisees, you will never enter the kingdom of heaven' (Matt. 5.20). This encouragement to reflect the exemplary dedication of scribes and Pharisees is difficult to reconcile with the fierce criticism of the scribes and Pharisees which Jesus seems to express later in the Gospel (Matt. 23.1–39).

The above-mentioned tensions within the Gospel of Matthew – more could be mentioned, but in this context I shall keep to the two that I have provided here as a short illustration – lead us to suppose that we need to reckon with a complicated process of composition. The Gospel was not written all at once, but in a number of stages.

Matthew begins close to Mark. In the first instance he follows the earliest Gospel. It is striking that he tells all the miracle stories in a notably briefer form. He does not deny that Jesus performed miracles, healed people of their diseases and freed them from the spirits that tormented them, but he attaches less importance to this than his fellow-evangelist. Matthew sees Jesus first of all as a special and creative 'rabbi': a teacher and scribe. With the tendency towards order which is so typical of him, Matthew has collected Jesus' teaching into five discourses. The first is the Sermon on the Mount (Matt. 5–7) and the last is the apocalyptic discourse, culminating in the pericope about the judgment that the Son of man will give (Matt. 24–25). It is also immediately clear what picture of Jesus is being painted here. He is the strict teacher who points out the seriousness of the situation to his disciples. In the description of the judgment we look in vain for the word 'grace' (Matt. 25.31–46). All human beings are judged by their specific actions.

Matthew adds hardly any elements that are of interest to us to the passion narrative that he found in the Gospel of Mark. The fact that Jesus died as a righteous sufferer on the cross can also be interpreted by Matthew as a 'suffering for others' (Matt. 20.28; 26.26–29), but does not detract from the seriousness of the warnings about judgment. Jesus' death on the cross is not a source of grace or reconciliation. Rather, the dramatic event bears the character of an 'example'. Anyone who chooses the way of Jesus can be confronted with torture and suffering. Those are the consequences of a choice which can prove to be of decisive significance for a person's life. It seems advisable to understand Matthew's interpretation of the name of Jesus at the beginning of his Gospel – 'he shall deliver his people from their sins' (Matt. 1.21) – in this framework. Jesus delivers people from sins by showing them the way that is characterized by 'excessive righteousness' (Matt. 5.20) and a love for others which is quite out of the ordinary (Matt. 5.48).

Is this the last word about Matthew's theological insights? Another reason for the complexity of the Gospel is the suggestion that while here we have a mainstream of his 'theology', alongside it we can indisputably find other subsidiary currents. So I think it not improbable that the Gospel has undergone one or more revisions. In the period after the destruction of the temple in Jerusalem, when the ways of Judaism and Christianity diverged radically, a revision took place which gave the original Gospel a more marked anti-Jewish character. The traces of this revision can be found above all in the second part of Matthew: the parable of the two sons (Matt. 21.28–32); the addition to the parable of the unjust steward which can be regarded as the beginning of the church's 'supersession theology', 'Therefore I tell you the kingdom of God will be taken away from you, and given to a nation producing the fruits of it' (Matt. 21.43); the notorious text which only appears in Matthew's account of the trial of Jesus, 'and all the people answered and said: His blood be on us and on our children' (Matt. 27.25); and finally the pericope which has become famous as 'the lies of the Jewish council' (Matt. 28.11–15). Against the background of this distance from Jewish tradition, we need no longer be surprised that the Gospel ends with the universal 'mission command':

Go and make disciples of all nations (Matt. 28.16–20).

Is that then definitively the last word on Matthew's 'theology'? There is a good reason not to answer this question in the affirmative immediately. There are a number of texts which seem to shed yet another light on the significance of Jesus Christ. It is no exaggeration to describe Matthew as the evangelist who is most influenced by the apocalyptic view of the world. Thus he takes over Jesus' apocalyptic discourse in Mark

13 almost completely and adds a few further elements to it –
especially the extended description of the judgment – which do
not diminish the apocalyptic sphere but actually reinforce it.
Completely in accord with the Jewish tradition, Matthew is the
only one of the evangelists to use the term 'kingdom of heaven'.
He is not consistent here, and that makes one think. In two
passages already mentioned – the parable of the two sons
(21.28–32) and the addition to the parable of the unjust
steward (Matt. 21.45) – he suddenly speaks of the kingdom of
God, and in so doing uses 'enter the kingdom of God' and 'the
kingdom of God shall be taken away' – which suggests that the
kingdom no longer lies hidden in the future but has already
become a reality in this world in one way or another. The text
mentioned above involuntarily suggests the Gospel of John – for
example the conversation between Jesus and Nicodemus in
John 3.3–5. That applies even more to another text:

> Come to me, all who labour and are heavy laden, and I will
> give you rest. Take my yoke upon you and learn from me; for
> I am gentle and lowly in heart, and you will find rest for your
> souls. For my yoke is easy and my burden is light (Matt.
> 11.28–30).

This is a different Jesus from the strict teacher of the Sermon on
the Mount and the apocalyptic discourse. The picture of Jesus
that is conjured up here is again strikingly similar to the way in
which the Fourth Gospel writes about him. Moreover there is a
good reason why this part, together with the passage that has
preceded it (Matt. 11.25–27), has been characterized in
scholarly literature as a 'Johannine thunderbolt'. So within one
Gospel the picture of Jesus has slowly but surely changed, and
his life and death have also taken on another meaning.

## Luke

The author of the Third Gospel – it seems not improbable that
the church tradition was right in calling him Luke – also used

Mark as a source, but he went to work in quite a different way from Matthew. Any reader of the Gospel of Luke will discover very quickly that the author is much less dependent on Mark than his fellow-evangelist. Luke does not hesitate to omit large sections and adds considerably more material than Matthew. The independence of the Third Evangelist already emerges from the verses with which he begins his work:

> Inasmuch as many have undertaken to compile a narrative of the things which have been accomplished among us, just as they were delivered to us by those who from the beginning were eyewitnesses and ministers of the word, it seemed good to me also, having followed all things closely for some time past, to write an orderly account for you, most excellent Theophilus, that you may know the truth concerning the things of which you have been informed (Luke 1.1–4).

These sentences make it possible for us to sketch a profile of the evangelist. He himself was not an eye-witness and thus did not belong to the circle of the first followers of Jesus. He is interested in the past, but does not seem to be content with the attempts that have already been made to put the events down in writing. Therefore he himself has engaged in an investigation and offers the results of his efforts to an authoritative person whom he addresses as 'most excellent Theophilus'.

The Gospel of Luke introduces readers to a social world which is different from that in the Gospels of Mark and Matthew. The scene has not changed: Jesus still goes through Galilee and at a particular moment sets off for Jerusalem, but a considerable number of those who are with him come from a different social class. Here are a couple of examples. There are some women in the company of Jesus who at all events belong to 'better circles' (Luke 8.1–3). The conversations with Pharisees often do not take place on the way, but at meals to which Jesus has received an invitation (Luke 11.37). So he also eats 'in the house of a ruler of the Pharisees' (Luke 14.1). On these occasions Jesus seems to have preferred to pass on his insights in the form of stories. These parables in the Gospel of Luke are also to a great degree set in a milieu of men with money and possessions: a rich man builds great barns (Luke 12.13–21); someone else who is also not without means is said to have arranged a great banquet and invited men who from the tone of their excuses belong among the rich in society (Luke 14.15–24); the parables of the prodigal son (Luke 15.11–32), the unjust steward (Luke 16.1–8) and the rich man and poor Lazarus (Luke 16.19–31) are unmistakably derived from the same social context.

Luke wrote a Gospel for well-to-do people. The poor are called blessed without qualification (Luke 6.20). They do not need to worry about entering the kingdom of God. After his death the poor Lazarus is taken to Abraham's bosom directly by angels (Luke 16.22). But what will happen to all these rich men? They are clearly warned: 'But woe to you rich, for you already have your consolation' (Luke 6.24). What can they do to avoid sharing the fate of the rich man who allows poor Lazarus to come to grief on his doorstep?

The answer to this question is so simple that readers have difficulty in believing their eyes: 'They have Moses and the prophets, let them hear them' (Luke 16.29). Moreover, later we even hear these words: 'If they do not hear Moses and the prophets, neither will they be convinced if some one should rise from the dead' (Luke 16.31). The question cannot be avoided: what is really the significance of the life and death of Jesus Christ in the light of these statements?

The evangelist Luke does not make it easy for us to answer this question in a satisfactory way. Here it is not impossible that our expectations are usually set too high. Theologians with almost two thousand years of church history and the history of dogma behind them have so many dogmatic systems running round in their heads, both consciously and unconsciously, that they have difficulty in reading the biblical texts in an open way.

The tone of the Gospel of Luke is unmistakably set in the birth narrative. Shepherds near Bethlehem are told:

> Be not afraid, for behold, I bring you good news of a great joy which will come to all the people;
> for to you this day is born a saviour (Luke 2.10–11).

Two terms may be said to be characteristic of the theological view in the Gospel of Luke: 'Spirit of God' and 'good tidings/ joy'. (a) The Spirit of God descends in bodily form on Jesus (Luke 3.22) and seems to accompany him on his way (Luke 4.1, 14, 18). After Pentecost, the same Spirit will be a source of inspiration for the Christian community (Acts 2.1–13). (b) It can be inferred from the text quoted above that the birth of Jesus is a reason for great joy on earth. But that is not all. A feast is also celebrated in heaven. We hear of good news and joy at the moment when a sinner is converted (Luke 15.7,10). With all this in mind we can now investigate the significance of regarding Jesus as the 'Saviour' – it is also possible to translate the term 'Redeemer'.

How does the 'saving work' of Jesus take place? In the synagogue in Nazareth he reads an evocative passage from the book of the prophet Isaiah:

> The Spirit of the Lord is upon me, because he has anointed me to preach good news to the poor (Luke 4.18 = Isa. 61.1).

Again the poor emphatically come into the picture. Moreover we need to note that Jesus in any case is addressing the poor and – I would add – all those who are among the pariahs of society and are not in a position to stand up for themselves: the blind, prisoners, widows and orphans (Luke 18.1–8). One cannot say that this is a new idea, since scripture and tradition argue no less ardently for the protection of the weak in society (cf. e.g. Ps. 72). From what has been said above it has become immediately clear that Jesus can also be called the 'saviour' of the rich, provided that they are ready to live from now on in accord with Moses and the prophets (Luke 16.29). Is Jesus finally also the Saviour because he died for our sins on the cross? Anyone who hopes to find this classical theological notion in the Gospel of Luke will look in vain. Luke describes the suffering and death of Jesus in a matter-of-fact way and he seems restrained in his theological interpretation. That is particularly evident in the section in which he relates Jesus' last supper with his disciples (Luke 22.14–23). He diverges from Mark and deliberately chooses expressions which are closely related to a eucharistic tradition on which the apostle Paul seems to be dependent (I Cor. 11.23–25). Through the eucharistic words of institution in the Gospel of Luke, too, the suffering of Jesus can be seen as a 'suffering for others'. The significance of this statement is brought out later in the Gospel. In contrast to the Gospels of Mark and Matthew, Jesus and his disciples do not go out to the Mount of Olives 'after they had sung a hymn' (Mark 14.26; Matt. 26.30); they continue to remain there and get involved in a series of conversations. It is abundantly clear that Luke has deliberately edited this part. Jesus instituted the eucharist. He characterized his suffering and dying as a 'suffering for you' (vv.19 and 20). What does that mean? Jesus gives the answer to this question during the closing conversations round the table. Luke has fundamentally changed the text from the Gospel of Mark in which Jesus says that he is 'giving his life as a ransom for many' (Mark 10.45; Matt. 20.28):

For which is the greater, one who sits at table or one who serves? Is it not the one who sits at table? But I am among you as one who serves (Luke 22.27).

It is not doing the Third Evangelist an injustice to say that this is the summary of his Gospel. Jesus saves because he has appeared 'as a servant'. So he has given the poor a new perspective and shows the rich how they can live: 'let the greatest among you become as the youngest, and the leader as one who serves' (Luke 22.26). If this advice were put into practice, then society would look totally different (cf. Luke 17.7–10).

Finally, Luke's description of the death of Jesus is also typical. In contrast to the Gospels of Mark and Matthew, in which Jesus cries for God's help and attention, here the struggle seems to be carried on quietly. Jesus' last words indicate his surrender to God:

> 'Father, into your hands I commend my Spirit.' And when he had said that, he gave up the spirit (Luke 23.46).

The reaction of the Roman centurion is no less striking:

> Truly this was a righteous man (Luke 23.47).

This sounds remarkable on the lips of a Roman soldier, but by the remark Luke, very much in the spirit of the Old Testament–Jewish tradition, will have meant that Jesus may be called 'righteous' because he lived and died in perfect loyalty to Moses and the prophets, the commandments of God.

# 7

# The Gospel of John

## A *variegated Gospel*

Can the Fourth Gospel add anything new to all that has already been said by the apostle Paul and the authors of the three Synoptic Gospels? In fact anyone who thinks that the most important aspects have now been fairly well illustrated is mistaken. The Fourth Gospel is the prime example of the variegated nature of the New Testament. In the chorus of voices of apostles and evangelists John's voice may not be harshly dissonant, but he does sing a new and surprising melody. Obviously agreements are to be noted with other New Testament writings. Sometimes there is some affinity in the choice of words and terms. John too uses terms like kingdom of God and Son of man, but for him they function in another framework. The Fourth Gospel knows a number of stories which also appear in the Synoptic Gospels. However, anyone who takes the trouble to make a close comparison will soon discover differences in presentation. In the Fourth Gospel a miracle story is almost always – the wedding at Cana is an exception to the rule (John 2.1–11) – followed by an extensive and often profound conversation in which the event proves to be the launching pad for complicated theological reflections. John's view of present and future is no less complex and 'ambiguous' than that of the apostle Paul. It could even be called more so, but presumably I have already said enough to make readers curious about this evangelist's view of the suffering and death of Jesus Christ.

## The key witness loses his authority

For centuries the words of the Fourth Gospel were listened to with great reverence. Already at an early stage of church history – second/third century – people thought it certain that the author belonged to the small circle of the first disciples. He was thought to be the man who is mentioned several times in the Gospel itself as 'the beloved disciple' (John 13.13; 20.2). He had a special position within the group of Jesus' followers. He appeared as Jesus' trusted friend and was the key witness to his death on the cross (John 19.25–27, 35–37).

It almost goes without saying that great importance was attached to his words. None of the other three evangelists had been so closely involved in events and John could present himself as the bosom friend of Jesus. Moreover, texts from the Fourth Gospel played a major role from the start of christological reflection in the first centuries of church history. Without these texts the classical confessional writings and dogmas would have been expressed in other words. Terms like 'pre-existence' (= the existence of the only-begotten Son of God before the creation of the world) and 'incarnation' (= the incarnation/the being made flesh of the Word/the Son) would have had a less prominent place in dogmatics.

Age-old Christian certainties slowly began to be shaken in the nineteenth century. Venerable traditions were looked on with critical eyes. Knowledge of the distant past increased, and the Bible became a book in which people related their experiences of God. Had the church tradition interpreted the relationship between the Fourth Evangelist and 'the beloved disciple' properly? Was the evangelist really concerned only with historical truth, with giving a reliable account of the events which had taken place in the recent past?

Space here does not allow us to discuss this question exhaustively, so I shall limit myself to one aspect. The Fourth Gospel clearly pays a good deal of attention to the conflict between Jesus and Judaism. Both parties are as it were daggers drawn with one another, and often the evangelist writes that the Jews were already busy carrying stones in order to stone their opponents in accord with the commandment in the Torah (John 8.59; 10.31). We must ask how far this is a historically reliable account of events in the time of Jesus. At all events, a comparison shows that this view of the past is hardly shared by the three other evangelists, if at all. What interest did John have in elucidating events in this way?

The Fourth Gospel presents a picture of Judaism which seems to fit much better the situation in the period shortly after the destruction of the temple in 70 CE. Clearly the author – consciously or unconsciously – is projecting the oppositions and conflicts of his own time back on to the life of Jesus. Throughout his work he emerges as a creative and profound theologian. He has interpreted and used the stories about Jesus which were in circulation in such a way that they can answer the questions that were alive in his community. He remained anonymous, but he presented himself as the key witness *par excellence* (John 19.35–37) – here it must be remembered that while he wanted to bear witness to the truth, for him the truth was far more than just a historical truth.

In 70 CE the Jerusalem temple was destroyed by Roman soldiers. That put an end to the revolt which had broken out in the country some years earlier. A majority of the Jewish population, their morale high, and stimulated by the political and religious ideals of the Zealots, had engaged in armed revolt against a Roman domination which was regarded as hostile to God.

While the blood of many thousands flowed – believers and brave men, fanatics and waverers, armed men and also the defenceless – God was silent. Nor did God intervene when a Roman soldier thoughtlessly threw a burning torch into the temple complex. After so many centuries it is still possible to have some idea of the consequences of this catastrophe. Countless people were killed in the conflicts, and others had sought a good outcome beyond the frontiers of Jewish territory. The economy was disrupted and in the religious sphere, too, rubble needed to be cleared away. Could Judaism survive without the temple in Jerusalem?

Johanan ben Zakkai, a scribe from Pharisaic circles, thought that he had discovered an answer which later generations also found meaningful. His view was that it was more necessary than ever to concentrate on observing the commandments of the Torah. Those who could no longer accept this in fact put themselves outside the circle of all those who wanted to adopt such a course. To the outsiders were assigned, in succession, those who had belonged to the party of the Sadducees, those who had joined the sect of the Essenes, those who still could not forget the ideals of the Zealots, and finally also the Jews who had become followers of Jesus Christ.

## Pre-existent wisdom

The Fourth Gospel unmistakably bears traces of this turbulent period of Jewish history. The author is putting his thoughts down at a time when, also as a result of the catastrophe, the ways of Judaism and Christianity were diverging increasingly. We do not know for certain who he was, nor can we say where he was living at that time. Church tradition mentioned Ephesus in Asia Minor, but my preference is for Alexandria in Egypt.

Many Jews had been living in this city for centuries – it might be called the New York of antiquity. Alexandria was also a religious melting pot. Here the great Jewish community could not avoid contact with those of different views, and it was subject to the influence of both Egyptian and Graeco-Hellenistic language and culture. So it was no coincidence that in the third century BCE the translation of the Hebrew Bible into Greek was put in hand in this city. The Jews in Alexandria did not live in isolation from Jerusalem, but in their specific situation they saw themselves compelled to express their belief in the God of Israel in a way which was also understandable for Jews who were alienated from their Hebrew heritage. Thus a bridge was built between the Jewish world and Hellenistic culture, a bridge which was later used gratefully by Christian preachers to take the gospel of Jesus Christ outside the frontiers of Jewish territory. Alexandria was a bustling centre of Jewish scholarship and culture. Stories from scripture and tradition were worked on and brought up to date orally and in writing. Thus the life of Moses was dramatized in a play written by a Jewish playwright of the second century BCE. In it the leader of the people at the time of the exodus from Egypt was put on a pedestal and thus literally 'praised to the skies'. Moses was given a place on the throne of God in heaven. There was also a good deal of interest in Old Testament books about Wisdom. In the footsteps of scripture and tradition people saw Wisdom as a personification of a divine property and did not hesitate to speak of her pre-existence (Prov. 8.22). Before the beginning of creation Wisdom had been a 'favourite child with God' (Prov. 8.30).

In the exciting cosmopolitan word of Alexandria in the second half of the first century CE there was also a Christian community – presumably a small one. Its members were for the most part of Jewish origin, but they had joined those who called themselves followers of Jesus Christ. They had found their way with pain and difficulty. There are sayings in the Fourth Gospel which could indicate that they were thrown out of the synagogue with violence (John 9.22; 16.2). Their choice of Christ had radically changed their lives: members of their families refused to receive them and old friends had suddenly become enemies. Had they made a good choice?

Anyone who wants to understand the Fourth Evangelist must realize that he lived in a situation like the one sketched out here. His Gospel is strikingly polemical in tone. Matthew, too, did not spare his Jewish fellow-countrymen, but the Fourth Gospel goes further and is not afraid of applying terms like enemies, darkness, world, hatred and even devil to them (John 8.37–47). The gulf between Judaism and Christianity was definitively seen as unbridgable. Matthew still made an attempt to persuade those who thought differently. The Fourth Evangelist no longer thought it worth while to make the effort. He bears witness to his view, and anyone who does not want to accept it is written off for good. John was no seeker of the truth; he knew the truth and had no doubts.

## Incarnation

The Gospel of John begins at a lofty level. The famous prologue takes the reader far back in time to the pre-existence of the Word (= Logos). 'In the beginning was the Word' (John 1.1). It is certainly no coincidence that the first words of the prologue of John conjure up memories of the beginning of the first book of the Bible: 'In the beginning God created heaven and earth' (Gen. 1.1). In the letter to the Colossians we already encountered the notion that the pre-existent Christ had been involved in the creation of 'all things' (Col. 1.16). The prologue of the Fourth Gospel knows a similar vision of the origin of heaven and earth. The creation came into being through the pre-existent Word: 'All things were made by him and without him was not anything made that was made' (John 1.3).

The letter to the community of Colossae can hardly be compared with the Fourth Gospel. Each writing has a different theological atmosphere. Therefore it is all the more striking that in the texts I have mentioned they seem to be so closely related. One attractive explanation of this is that they have their roots in the same theological tradition. Some time before the beginning of our era there was already great interest in wisdom as a personified characteristic of God, above all in Jewish Hellenistic circles, and especially in Alexandria in Egypt. These philosophical speculations emerged from the text in the book of Proverbs which has already been mentioned. There wisdom speaks, among others, the following words:

The Lord created me
as the beginning of his wayys,
the first of his acts of old (Prov. 8.22).

The prologue of John is an imposing text. The evangelist will have made use of an already existing 'hymn' about the pre-existent Word. He worked on this hymn and adapted it. In this way he created a glittering beginning. Starting from the speculations about the Word (Logos /Wisdom) which were known in his circles, he leads his readers as it were imperceptibly to Jesus Christ – the name is mentioned for the first time only at the end of the prologue (John 1.17). Also under the influence of the apocryphal wisdom writing which bears the name of Jesus Sirach (or Ecclesiasticus), the conviction gained ground in early Jewish literature that it makes sense to identify pre-existent wisdom with the Torah. Of course this identification is obvious: those are wise who walk in the ways of the Lord, and precisely what those ways are can only be inferred from the commandments of the Torah. The prologue of the Gospel of John does not reject this notion out of hand completely, but does emphasize that it is not the Torah but Jesus Christ who is the incarnate Word (John 1.17).

One famous – or perhaps, given all the dogmatic disputes to which the text has given rise, we should call it notorious – sentence in the prologue is essential for a good understanding of the christology of the Fourth Gospel:

> The Word was made flesh
> and dwelt among us
> and we beheld his glory,
> a glory as of the only-begotten of the Father,
> full of grace and truth (John 1.14).

The text calls for a brief exposition – and here I shall leave out of account the role that these words have played in the formulation of the classical doctrine of the two natures of Christ. In the framework of this study we are not concerned with the problems of the person of Christ but with his work, soteriology. Therefore I shall now consider the question: what does this text say about the meaning that the Fourth Gospel attaches to the life and death of Jesus Christ?

At all events it seems necessary to speak of Jesus in quite a complex way. 'Flesh' and 'glory' come together in him in a manner which is not described more closely. So it is not strange to read that Jesus was 'wearied with his journey' (John 4.6). He was a man of flesh and blood, and in due course human beings become weary. To this degree the picture that the Fourth Evangelist sketches of Jesus does not differ fundamentally from that in the three Synoptic Gospels. That changes the moment he writes 'we have see his glory'. The term 'glory' unmistakably points towards God. There can be no doubt about that. God's glory becomes visible in this man. At the end of the story about the marriage of Cana this aspect returns unambiguously: 'This, the first of his signs, Jesus did at Cana in Galilee, and manifested his glory; and his disciples believed in him' (John 2.11).

John not only begins on a lofty level; he also makes salvation begin at an early stage. Paul concentrates wholly on the cross and the crucified Jesus. The three Synoptic Gospels showed more interest in the life of Jesus, but here they were less consistent than the author of the Fourth Gospel. For him, the cross is not the most important thing, but the incarnation. From the moment that 'the Word became flesh', the 'glory of God' is visible in the world, the light shines in darkness and 'grace and truth' have made their entry into earthly reality.

## Image of God

The world lies in darkness, humankind is dominated by sin and death. An unbridgable gulf divides earth from heaven. Human beings are infinitely far from God; they no longer have a clear and inspiring picture of God and, driven by despair, trust in idols, surrogate gods, caricatures of the God of Israel. Without being aware of it, by so doing they make themselves increasingly slaves of dark powers. The last sentence of the prologue of the Fourth Gospel sketches out this desperate situation in a few words: 'No one has seen God at any time . . .' (John

1.18). Is there nothing for us but a hopeless existence and unbridgable gulf?

John does not accept this conclusion. What comes after the sentence at the end of the prologue offers a surprising perspective and sums up briefly but powerfully the significance of the coming of Christ into this world: '. . . the only-begotten Son who is in the bosom of the Father, he has made him known'. In the human being Jesus, the glory of God has already become visible. Thus despite everything the light shines in the darkness and we can talk of salvation in this world. The incarnate Word paves the way to God.

Once more the Fourth Evangelist shows that he is an extraordinary creative theologian. As we saw, the metaphor of 'the bosom of the Father' is not unknown in early Jewish tradition: with a reference to Prov. 8.30 it is applied to the pre-existence of both Wisdom and the Torah. On the basis of this relationship – special, because it is intimate – they are in a position to reveal God's will and could therefore be seen as be seen as concrete forms of his love and faithfulness.

John brings the tradition up to date on the basis of his christological presuppositions. The consequence of the coming of Jesus Christ into the world – the Son sent by the Father (John 3.17) is that the specific functions of Wisdom and Torah are now transferred to him. In the life of Jesus Christ, salvation has taken concrete form: hands and feet in the literal sense of the word. He was the embodiment of the Father's love and faithfulness. Therefore, according to the Fourth Evangelist, he forms the climax in God's revelation. The Son is the most complete 'explanation' of the Father; he is the unique and original 'exegete' of God. Some chapters later the evangelist can therefore attribute the following words to Jesus: 'He who has seen me has seen the Father; how can you say, "Show us the Father?"' (John 14.9).

## Son of God

From earliest times the title Son of God was associated with terms like election, faithfulness and obedience: in relation to Israel, his elect people, God showed himself to be a faithful father who thought that he could expect equal faithfulness and obedience from his son (Ex. 4.22; Hos. 11.3). The Fourth Gospel is also familiar with such notions, but they are vastly overshadowed by the notion of uniqueness: Jesus is the Son of God *par excellence*. The result is that the evangelist attaches great importance to the unity of Father and Son, of God and Jesus Christ (John 12.44–50). In the dispute over christological dogma in the third and fourth centuries this unity is interpreted as a 'unity of substances or natures': God from God, light from light, true God from true God, begotten not made, *of the same substance as the Father*.

Was that the unity that John had in mind? There is no doubt that he attached great importance to the unity between God and Jesus Christ, but the notion of a 'unity of substance' does not appear in his Gospel, and one also looks in vain for the word 'nature'. Father and Son are one because they are one in spirit, one in will, one in their love for human beings, kindred spirits in their striving to rescue the world from the power of darkness (John 3.16–21).

However many qualifications the Fourth Evangelist may have wanted to make, in his own work he could not prevent 'the glory of God' overshadowing the humanity of Jesus – the flesh. In the end John does not describe Jesus as the human 'Son of God' who follows a course about which he sometimes has misgivings but which often takes him by surprise. In the Fourth Gospel there is no story about Jesus' doubt and anguish in the garden of Gethsemane (Mark 14.32–42). John's Jesus does not doubt, because he knows (John 12.23–28; 13.1). He knows the will of the Father and he goes the way of suffering in the calm, indeed cheerful, certainty that God will not let go of the initiative. For this reason there is no tragedy in the passion narrative in the Fourth Gospel. Even at his arrest Jesus takes control: he knows what awaits him and goes forward without fear. Temple police and soldiers fall to earth as one; however, Jesus does not opt for flight but in fact arrests himself (John 18.1–11).

The Fourth Gospel gives us the first model of a 'christology from above'. It is not the human being Jesus of Nazareth who is the focus of attention but the pre-existent Son of God who descends to earth from heaven, 'from above', and later returns to heaven. To avoid possible misunderstandings I should once again point out in passing that for the Fourth Gospel the confession of the oneness of God and Jesus, Father and Son, is in the first place focussed on the fact that both are one in their desire to save human beings and the world (John 3.16–21).

## Unique

The Fourth Evangelist's view of the significance of Jesus Christ can be summed up adequately with the word that I have put at the head of this section: he is absolutely unique, irreplaceable, and cannot be compared with anything or anyone. He is the only-begotten Son of God (John 7.28–29). No one else is like him. He is the light of the world (John 8.12) and himself speaks the words of God. He knows the truth and embodies it in all his actions. There is no doubt that for the Fourth Evangelist the notion of uniqueness was a condition of speaking responsibly about the life and death of Jesus.

The only-begotten Son of God alone may be thought to be in a position to point the way to the Father (John 14.4–11). Anyone who cannot accept that, opposes God's truth and takes the side of the lie. The Fourth Evangelist does not accept any compromises. He compels his readers to make a choice. He knows no other colours than black and white; tones of grey were unknown to him. There is no twilight on the frontier of light and darkness; in principle, between truth and lies there is only a deep, unbridgable gulf.

For this reason the Gospel of John provokes irritation even

now. Anyone who wants to defend Christian truth without hesitation against those who think otherwise will read this Gospel with much pleasure; however, those who abhor polemic and want to confront adherents of other religions and convictions in a balanced and tolerant way will have great difficulty with many passages in John. The past of the church speaks volumes here. More than once John's texts have been forged into weapons to challenge the faith of others with fire and sword. If it is indeed true that Jesus is the only way to God, then it must be concluded, for example, that the Jewish tradition has become insignificant and that the same needs to be said of all other religious convictions. In Jesus God has revealed himself once and for all. Anyone who wants to come to know God can do so only through the words and deeds of Jesus. His way is the truth: 'I am the way and the truth and the life; no one comes to the Father but by me' (John 14.6).

## The cross

After all that has been said, the question remains what significance John attached to the suffering and death of Jesus Christ. It will emerge that once again the evangelist adopts surprising courses. Of course he can no longer speak in the same way as Paul about the cross and the crucified Jesus. Anyone who attaches so much importance to the incarnation becomes somewhat perplexed when reflecting on the 'theology' of the passion narrative. Moreover, there can be no question of a *theologia crucis* in the spirit of Paul. The source of salvation and redemption is not Golgotha but the incarnate Word. Words like 'reconciliation' and 'atonement' do not occur in the Gospel of John, but one could say that the incarnation builds a bridge, removes the alienation between God and human beings, and overcomes hostility. Thus two parties which were at odds with one another are reconciled. Thanks to the fact that 'the glory of the Father' has become visible in the man Jesus, as the Son, the way of God has been paved anew for all those who believe.

What does the cross add to all this? A little and yet a great deal. John does not describe the suffering and death of Jesus as the absolute nadir on the way that he had to go. That, for example, is the direction taken by the impressive Christ hymn which Paul has quoted in his letter to the community in Philippi: 'And being found in human form he humbled himself and became obedient unto death, even death on a cross' (Phil. 2.8). Unlike Paul, John directs his attention not downwards – to symbolize this 'humiliation' – but 'upwards', as a sign of exaltation:

> And as Moses lifted up the serpent in the wilderness, so must the Son of man be lifted up, that whoever believes in him may have eternal life (John 3.14).

Anyone who is hung on a cross is indeed 'lifted up' in the literal sense of the word. It will become clear that Paul, who more than anyone else felt the scandal of the cross, could never ever have envisaged this notion. In the Fourth Gospel the concreteness of the suffering on the cross is completely sacrificed in favour of a theological view of the event. The cross becomes the crown of the work that was begun with the incarnation. That is underlined when John sums up the suffering and death of Jesus like this: 'The hour has come for the Son of man to be glorified' (John 12.23). Jesus' last words on the cross disclose the consummation of the work of redemption: 'It is finished' (John 19.30).

## The lamb of God

I could be accused of incompleteness if I did not discuss one more point. Only in the Fourth Gospel does the famous remark of John the Baptist occur:

> Behold, the lamb of God, that takes away the sins of the world (John 1.29, 36).

Anyone who conscientiously ventures to interpret these words will again discover that exegetes come – and on the basis of a close analysis of the text indeed have to come – to conclusions which are in tension with views which for centuries have dominated both dogmatic reflection and liturgy.

For dogma and liturgy Jesus is the lamb of God who allows himself voluntarily to be led away to the slaughter. Therefore his death on the cross has to be characterized as a sacrificial death. Through the blood of the lamb which is sacrificed, the sins of the world are taken away and reconciliation between God and human beings is brought about.

Was John the Baptist aware of all this when he pointed to Jesus and called him the lamb of God? That seems impossible to believe. There are no texts in the three Synoptic Gospels which even suggest that John the Baptist spoke about Jesus in this way. But even if we assume that the Fourth Evangelist put these words in the mouth of John the Baptist – and that was certainly the case – it is legitimate to ask precisely what he intended and whether he would really agree with the way in which the metaphor of Jesus as the lamb of God has been interpreted in church history and the history of dogma.

What was the evangelist thinking of when he wrote these words? Anyone who tries to give an exegetical rather than a dogmatic answer to this question will encounter much uncertainty, and discover that a satisfactory solution can be formulated only with great hesitation. At all events it must be thought improbable that the evangelist wanted to make any connection with the ritual of the Day of Atonement. The 'taking away' or 'carrying off' of the sins of the world could certainly point in that direction, but in this connection the Torah does not speak of a lamb but of a *goat* which, laden – symbolically – with the transgressions of the people of Israel, was taken into the wilderness and let loose there (Lev. 16.20–22).

The Gospel itself seems to want to point readers towards the Passover lamb. But here too we must consider whether if we follow this pointer, we are not too easily going in the wrong direction. According to a not unimportant exegetical tradition, in his description of the suffering and death of Jesus, the evangelist deliberately alludes to the Passover lamb twice.

The first time is when in his account of the interrogation of Jesus by Pontius Pilate he interrupts the course of his account with an indication of time: 'Now it was the day of Preparation of the Passover; it was about the sixth hour' (John 19.14). That means that it is the middle of the day preceding the evening celebration of the Passover and the Seder meal (I cannot discuss the chronological problem posed by the differences between the three Synoptic Gospels on the one hand and the Gospel of John on the other). During the 'Preparation for the Passover' many hundreds of lambs were slaughtered in the Jerusalem temple, which were eaten by the thousands of pilgrims and inhabitants of Jerusalem at the Seder meal that evening. On this day Jesus was scourged (John 19.1) and interrogated by Pontius Pilate, but it is difficult to demonstrate whether John also wants to make a theological connection between the two events. The torture and interrogation of Jesus does not take place in the temple but in the hall of judgment, which the Jewish leaders did not enter so as not to make themselves unclean (John 19.28). When Pontius Pilate points to Jesus, as John the Baptist did earlier, he calls him king and not lamb of God – such a term is unthinkable on the lips of the Roman procurator (John 19.14).

A second allusion to the Passover lamb could be conjectured in John's description of the crucifixion of Jesus. After the soldiers who have carried out the execution note that Jesus is already dead, they decide not to break his legs (John 19.33). The evangelist sees this as as the fulfilment of a word of scripture: 'not a bone of his shall be broken' (John 19.36). It is not completely certain which particular saying from scripture John had in mind. It could be that he wanted to refer to the Passover lamb. In the Torah we find instructions that the legs of the Passover lamb must not be broken (Ex. 12.40), but it is equally conceivable that he was thinking of a sentence from the Psalms: 'He keeps all his bones; not one of them is broken'

(Ps. 34.21). In my view there is most to be said for this latter possibility. Nowhere in the Old Testament–Jewish tradition is the Passover lamb described as the lamb of God, nor is there a mention of the Passover lamb which could take away the sins of the world.

The consequence of all this is in that in the end there is still one other possibility. In all probability, with the statement 'Behold the lamb of God which takes away the sins of the world' the evangelist wanted to evoke the picture of the suffering Servant of the Lord (Isa. 53). The two terms seem related in more than one respect – thus in Aramaic there is even a word which associates 'lamb' with 'servant'. Moreover it is said of the Servant of the Lord not only that he 'has taken our sickness and our pains upon himself' – the Septuagint even uses the rendering 'sins' (Isa. 53.4) – but also that he can be compared with 'a lamb which is led to the slaughter' (Isa. 53.7).

To avoid any misunderstandings let me add one further remark. Readers of the Gospel of John need constantly to be aware that all words, images and metaphors have their function within the framework of a christological reflection which is very conscious of the consequences of the choices that are being made. That also applies to the metaphor of the lamb of God. The presupposition that it could refer to a sacrificial animal that is being slaughtered takes no account of the theological context of the Gospel. The word 'blood' does not occur at all in the statement which the Fourth Gospel attributes to John the Baptist. Within the same context of the Gospel it is equally improbable that in using the term 'lamb of God' the evangelist was thinking of humiliation or of a defenceless lamb being led to the slaughter. Such an approach does not fit in with his christological view. Jesus does not go to Golgotha like a victim, but deliberately accepts his suffering and death. He is not humiliated on the cross, but at this place he is lifted up and glorified.

The saying about 'taking away the sins of the world' stands at the beginning of the Gospel and is not explicitly connected with the cross. That may be said to be evocative and is typical of John's view of the central significance of the incarnation. The cross completes and crowns the work of Jesus. Soteriologically speaking, nothing is created on Golgotha which was not there before. The taking away of the sins of the world already begins directly on the incarnation of the Word. It is not necessary here to wait for the death of Christ on the cross.

The incarnate Word shifts the frontier between present and future. John has departed radically from traditional Jewish apocalyptic notions about a kingdom of God or a messianic kingdom which still lies completely hidden in the future and which will soon be revealed. John's view can be described as 'realized eschatology'. Salvation is already present, and the kingdom of God is not something for the future. It has only to be discovered, sought and found, recognized and seen. For that, belief and a knowledge of what is happening are necessary. Those who have come to believe in Christ live within this dark world in the circle of light produced by God's love and grace. They no longer need to fear the judgment because they have been born again 'from above'; they may enter the kingdom of God (John 3.3–5) and have a part in eternal life (John 3.16–21).

Thus Jesus points the way for believers. He is the witness who can speak of heaven on earth (John 3.12). He creates knowledge and insight. He also gives his disciples an example of how they have to act and live (John 13.15). John wrote his Gospel to make all this clear to his community – a selection, but enough to give a good picture of Jesus:

Now Jesus did many other signs in the presence of the disciples, which are not written in this book; but these are written that you may believe that Jesus is the Christ, the Son of God, and that believing you may have life in his name (John 20.30–31).

## Still topical?

The author of the Fourth Gospel was an expert in scripture and tradition. Moreover he was a creative thinker, a man who seemed to be in a position to select from the religious melting pot of Alexandria those words, concepts and images which he could use to make the significance of Jesus Christ clear to his small community. Moses was highly respected in Jewish Hellenistic circles; the evangelist shows that Jesus Christ towered far above him (John 1.17). Speculations about the pre-existent Wisdom were popular. John thought that he could put an end to all discussions by making a simple identification: Jesus Christ is the embodiment of this Wisdom; he is the incarnate Word.

From a christological perspective John was playing for high stakes. For him it was all or nothing. He did not introduce any nuances, nor did he create any room for other notions. For centuries his Gospel was a source of inspiration to a church which thought it owned not only wisdom but also the truth.

John was polemical and drew boundaries. Given his situation, that was presumably the only way to keep his small community in the great city of Alexandria on its feet. Over against the views and claims of the Jewish tradition and other convictions he powerfully argued that Christian faith was right. Can we now, nineteen centuries later, repeat what evidently needed to be said then? Those who think that they have to answer the question affirmatively put great obstacles in the way of dialogue with adherents of other views. Those who have the courage to answer that it can never be the purpose of the Bible to use words as weapons will look for elements in the message of John which continue to inspire them despite everything: Jesus as an image of God, the embodiment of God's love and grace; he pointed a way to a God whom he had come to know as a Father – he bore witness to this God and he trusted in this God so much that he was not even afraid to look the dark powers of this world straight in the eye.

## Letters of John

It is impossible to take leave of the Fourth Evangelist without considering the three letters in the New Testament which also bear the name of John. Whether we have to do with same author is a question which we shall be discussing later. The content of these writings is such that only the first letter is important for us.

The Gospel of John is not only difficult for people in our time to understand; the first letter of John shows that the Gospel already gave rise to misunderstandings in the first century. This makes it necessary to explain particular aspects more closely and to provide some commentary. Moreover I John seems more like a theological treatise than an authentic letter. It is even possible to classify it as a 'pastoral message' or a 'sermon'. A series of admonitions runs through the whole work like a scarlet thread (1.15–17; 3.11–24; 4.7–12; 4.19–5.3). The author knows that the community risks being torn apart by oppositions. In this situation he makes an extreme effort to preserve unity by pointing to the heart of the Christian confession.

The beginning of I John – the 'prologue' of the letter (I John 1.1–4) – will immediately remind all readers of the prologue to the Fourth Gospel (John 1.1–18). That is also precisely what the author of the letter wants to achieve. He begins with the gospel and sums that up in a couple of sentences. But then he goes further and looks at the concrete situation in the community. He writes polemically and does not mince his words. He bluntly points out a great failing. Fine words are spoken, but in everyday practice there is little left of the high-flown language (I John 1.5–2.2). The writer hammers home one and the same message: faith and doing God's commandments belong indissolubly together (I John 2.3–6). Those who talk of 'walking in the light' and 'the love of God' but have no concern for the brothers and sisters within the community are called liars (I John 2.4). Faith without concrete 'brotherly love', which does not take action to secure justice and righteousness (I John 3.7) and is not concerned about the fate of the poor (I John 3.17), is quite unthinkable (I John 2.7–11; 3.11–17).

This sets the tone for the letter. Those who suppose, on the basis of a misunderstanding of the Fourth Gospel, that they can live with their heads in the clouds are given a rude awakening and have both their feet firmly placed on the ground. The polemical character of I John does not make reading the letter unalloyed pleasure. Its theme is limited, and the way in which it is treated is neither varied nor imaginative. Although views about authorship diverge, not least because of what I have just said I cannot really imagine that the author of the Fourth Gospel also composed the letter.

Of course the language and style of the two works show many affinities, but quite important differences in content can be noted. In contrast to the Gospel, in the letter attention is fixed emphatically and often on the speedy return of Jesus Christ (I John 2.20; 3.2; 4.17). In this connection false teachers who disturb the community are described as 'anti-Christs' (I John 2.18, 22; 4.3) – a notion that is derived from both Jewish and early Christian apocalyptic expectations of the future (Mark 13.6, 22).

But there is more than this, and here we enter the subject-matter of the present book. The false teachers in the letter, the author's opponents, seem to be denying the incarnation (I John 4.2; 5.6). They put so much emphasis on the divine character of the Word that they can no longer imagine that the Christ, the Son of God, could have allied himself with the man Jesus of Nazareth (I John 2.2; 4.15; 5.5, 10). It is impossible here to look in detail at the theological background to such notions. But it is certain that here we come upon Gnostic ideas. The negative view of the bodily as part of anti-godly matter results in a 'docetic' christology: the incarnation of the Word, the incarnation of the Son of God, did not really take place; Christ was only 'apparently' an authentic human being.

The author of I John is anything but a Gnostic. Faith is concrete. The incarnation is a reality. In Jesus, Christ has become a man of flesh and blood (I John 5.6). It seems legitimate to pre-suppose that this concern to leave no doubt whatsoever about the concreteness of the human nature of Jesus Christ is the explanation of the remarkable fact that the letter, unlike the Fourth Gospel, speaks of 'the blood of Jesus' (I John 1.7). The suffering of Jesus, too, was real suffering; blood really flowed. The author unmistakably thinks in cultic terms: 'the blood of Jesus cleanses us from all sins' (I John 1.7; cf.3.3), and therefore in the end he can call Jesus Christ 'the expiation for our sins' (I John 2.2; 4.10). Do these statements allude to the ritual of the Day of Atonement? The cultic terminology seems to point in this direction. At all events, I John builds a bridge to the letter to the Hebrews.

# 8

# The Letter to the Hebrews

## Disputed

In the list of New Testament works there are some letters which strictly speaking cannot be regarded as letters. In the last section of the previous chapter we have already come across such a work which is difficult to define: I John – more a theological treatise or sermon than a letter. The same can be said of the book of the Bible which we now need to consider. In this 'letter', too, the writer comes straight to the point. He does not give his name and says nothing about his antecedents. Who is he? It seems impossible to discover his identity. Around a century ago a prominent theologian and historian argued that the letter could have been written by a woman. He had arrived at this idea because the famous list of courageous witnesses to the faith in the eleventh chapter of the letter speaks respectfully of the persistence of women in the faith. Prisca or Priscilla could be a possible author. She was married to Aquila and was probably of Jewish descent (Acts 18.2). Paul knew her well and had a high opinion of her (I Cor. 16.19; Rom. 16.3–4). Those who find this notion attractive can confidently adopt it. They are hardly likely to be proved wrong.

Sometimes the name of Apollos also crops up in the long list of possible authors of the letter. In the Acts of the Apostles, Apollos is introduced like this: 'Now a Jew named Apollos, a native of Alexandria, came to Ephesus. He was an eloquent man, well versed in the scriptures' (Acts 18.24). The profile of the author of Hebrews conjured up by the text shows some agreements with the biographical data of Apollos. The letter is written by a scribe who knew his job. That may be concluded from the large number of references to passages from the Old Testament. The way in which scripture is interpreted suggests that the spiritual background of the author must be sought in Hellenistic Jewish circles. In the previous chapter about the Gospel of John we noted that in such a case it is natural to look towards Alexandria in Egypt. So was Apollos indeed the author of Hebrews? It is tempting to speculate that he was, but this cannot be more than a conjecture. The author of the letter to the Hebrews remains anonymous.

In the first centuries of Christianity the uncertainty about authorship meant that the letter was not accepted as canonical by the whole church. The hesitations which already existed were reinforced by a passage which would have led to great tension in the early Christian church had it been really taken seriously.

> For it is impossible to restore again to repentance those who have once been enlightened, who have tasted the heavenly gift, and have become partakers of the Holy Spirit, and have tasted the goodness of the word of God and the powers of the age to come, and then commit apostasy, since they crucify the son of God on their own account and hold him up to contempt (Heb. 6.4–6).

We have to conclude from this text that a second repentance is ruled out. Anyone who is converted to Christianity and then leaves the Christian community – for example for fear of persecution and martyrdom – can never return to the church. The author of this letter formulates his view so clearly that no other interpretation is possible. Above all in the first centuries of Christianity this situation repeatedly occurred in times of great persecution. Not everyone is born to be a martyr. It seems legitimate to ask whether such a passionate and inexorable standpoint is in accord with the good news, the gospel, once preached by Jesus of Nazareth. In my view the answer to this question is an easy one.

## Confident in faith

This objectionable text does not stand in isolation. The earnest, strict words breathe the atmosphere in which the letter to the Hebrews was written. We can only guess at the exact time and place of composition. The writer is very reticent when it comes to concrete information. In the final chapter the name of Timothy, Paul's well-known colleague and companion, suddenly appears (Heb. 15.23), and a greeting is brought from 'the brothers from Italy' (Heb. 15.24). Was the letter written in Italy – or Rome? – by someone from Paul's circle? We do not know. When the canonicity of the letter became an issue, its apostolicity was guaranteed by attributing it to Paul, but already in the Middle Ages experts on the scriptures thought that this was impossible. The letter to the Hebrews is quite different from the letters that Paul was accustomed to write and – what is more important – considerable theological differences can also be noted. The letter was written at a time when the first persecutions had been survived and a new generation of Christians had gained the upper hand in the community. Time went on, and slowly but surely the original enthusiasm declined. That was even more the case when it was increasingly difficult for Christians to maintain their social respectability. We are not yet at the time of the great persecutions of Christians which broke out for the first time at the end of the first century – rather, we have merely incidental expressions of anger and hatred, as for example in 64, when the emperor Nero used the Christians as scapegoats after the great fire which reduced part of Rome to ashes.

The community to which the letter is written has not been persecuted, but it is bearing the burden of being disciples of Jesus. There is a great danger that many people will lose courage. That is why the letter has been written. It is a theological treatise with an extremely practical focus. Central to it is the question of the consequences of Christian faith for everyday life. All its profound theological reflections are ultimately meant only to provide a firm foundation for pastoral advice. The author wants above all to present an encouraging argument. That is why he devotes so much attention to the stories about witnesses to the faith in the Old Testament. They, too, were confronted with setbacks and opposition, with persecutions and martyrdom, but they did not lose courage. Their faith was so strong that they remained faithful to God and, firmly believing in God, accepted the consequences of their conviction. Their 'exemplary' faith is a source of inspiration. Thus the author proves to have a soft heart. They are not alone in their struggle for faith. They are 'surrounded by a great cloud of witnesses'. The long summary of all those who did not deny their faith despite all that they experienced ends with this encouraging thought. I shall go on to quote the concluding sentences, not just because they may be thought to be typical, but because they are a good introduction to the next section, in which I shall look for an answer to the question of what view Hebrews has of the meaning of the suffering of Jesus Christ:

> Therefore, since we are surrounded by so great a cloud of witnesses, let us also lay aside every weight, and sin which clings so closely, and let us run with perseverance the race that is set before us, looking to Jesus the pioneer and perfecter of our faith, who for the joy that was set before him endured the cross, despising the shame, and is seated at the right hand of the throne of God (Heb. 12.1–2).

## Solidarity

Above all, the beginning of the letter to the Hebrews conjures up memories of the Gospel of John. Once again readers are expected to be able to think on two levels. Here too Jesus is called the Son 'whom He (= God) appointed the heir of all things, through whom he also created the world' (Heb. 1.2). The evangelist John went on to attach great importance to the incarnation of the Word (John 1.14). So too does the author of the letter to the Hebrews. Of course he does not use precisely the same terminology, but he emphasizes the incarnation of the Son with the same force. A close comparison of Hebrews and John soon shows that each interprets the humanity of Jesus in its own way. 'The Word was made flesh,' John writes, and at one point he gives Jesus a human feature – the weary man by the well (John 4.6) – but in the passion narrative the humanity virtually fades into the background, because the evangelist wants to express the sovereignty of Jesus' knowledge. Hebrews puts the emphasis elsewhere. The author emphatically associates the humanity of Jesus with his suffering and death on the cross. He does so in a way which recalls the accounts of Jesus' wrestling in the garden of Gethsemane in the Synoptic Gospels:

> In the days of his flesh, Jesus offered up prayers and supplications, with loud cries and tears, to him who was able to save him from death, and he was heard for his godly fear. Although he was a son, he learned obedience through what he suffered (Heb. 5.7–8).

In his life and death Jesus was engaged in a human struggle. He was not remote from us, because he already knew everything, but in his typically human emotions he comes close to our own vulnerable humanity. His eyes filled with tears, just as we too can shed bitter tears. He prayed to God for help, just as we too pray for changes to our lives. He knew anxiety, just as our life can come to be dominated by fear and worry. He had to learn the meaning of obedience to God through malice and shame, as we constantly have to. Jesus knows about human existence from his own experience. He knows what it is to be human. This 'solidarity' is the source of our salvation. The author expresses these thoughts in a couple of texts which are closely related. Because they are so important, I shall quote them:

> Since therefore the children share in flesh and blood, he (= Jesus) himself likewise partook of the same nature, that

through death he might destroy him who has the power of death, that is, the devil, and deliver all those who through fear of death were subject to lifelong bondage.

For surely it is not with angels that he is concerned but with the descendants of Abraham. Therefore he had to be made like his brethren in every respect, so that he might become a merciful and faithful high priest in the service of God, to make expiation for the sins of the people. For because he himself has suffered and been tempted, he is able to help those who are tempted (Heb. 2.14–18).

For we have not a high priest who is unable to sympathize with our weaknesses, but one who in every respect has been tempted as we are, yet without sinning (Heb. 4.15).

The evangelist John spoke about Jesus in a complex way. So too does the author of Hebrews. Readers may be certain of Jesus' solidarity. He was a human being as we are, with all those feelings and emotions that we know; with all the anxieties and uncertainties which are not alien to us; with all the lures which lead us into temptation. And it is over this last point that the cardinal difference comes to light. Where others 'sin' – in other words cannot and will not resist temptations sufficiently – Jesus did not 'sin', because he remained faithful to God, despite everything that happened to him.

The letter to the Hebrews does not draw readers' attention exclusively to Jesus' humanity. That is abundantly clear from the text quoted above. Our gaze is quite deliberately directed upwards, towards heaven. That is where Jesus is now, and there he fulfils a vital function for us. He has 'set himself at the right hand of the majesty on high' (Heb. 1.3; 8.1; 12.3). Yet he knows what it is to be a human being on earth.

## Jesus as high priest

The New Testament uses a large number of images, notions, titles and metaphors in connection with Jesus. He is scribe and teacher; he is rabbi and Christ; he is living water and living bread; he is shepherd and vine; he is light and life; he is Son of God and Son of man; he comes from above and returns to his Father's house; he is Lord and Saviour; he is the one who is to come who sits in heaven at the right hand of the Father. Evangelists and apostles made intensive use of the Old Testament tradition in order to express the significance of Jesus with the help of existing terms and metaphors. A great deal proved possible, but not everything helped to clarify matters. The New Testament authors were remarkably restrained in making comparisons with the temple cult in Jerusalem. On closer inspection the cautious distance is less strange than it might perhaps seem at first sight. Paul wrote letters to communities which had a considerable number of Gentile Christian members. Comparisons with the temple cult would have increased rather than reduced the already existing confusion. Each in his own way, the evangelists preserved the recollection that Jesus' activity took place more outside the temple than in it. It is virtually impossible to pass a definite judgment on Jesus' view of the cult, but it seems difficult to deny that he criticized current practices.

One New Testament writing is a great exception to all this, and that is the letter to the Hebrews. Not only is Jesus called 'high priest', but the Old Testament cultic regulations also appear at length. For a better understanding of what follows it is important once again to emphasize that here we have a metaphor. The function which Jesus fulfils in the relationship between God and human beings is compared with that of the high priest who similarly appears as an intermediary, a 'mediator' (Heb. 8.6; 9.15; 12.24) between God and the people of Israel. I have already mentioned in an earlier chapter that this special function of the high priest emerged above all at the celebration of the Day of Atonement (Lev. 16). There is no mistaking the fact that the author of the Letter to the Hebrews gives pride of place to this:

So that he might become a merciful and faithful high priest in the service of God, to make expiation for the sins of the people (Heb. 2.17).

The extended metaphor which is subsequently developed in the letter needs to be interpreted against this same Old Testament–Jewish background. Here is a text which may be regarded as the heart of the matter:

Consequently he (= Jesus) is able for all time to save those who draw near to God through him, since he always lives to make intercession for them. For it was fitting that we should have such a high priest, holy, blameless, unstained, separated from sinners, exalted above the heavens. He has no need, like those high priests, to offer sacrifices daily, first for his own sins and then for those of the people; he did this once and for all when he offered up himself (Heb. 7.25–28).

This passage forms the climax of the christology of the letter to the Hebrews. Jesus can be compared with a high priest in the Old Testament–Jewish tradition. That is the conclusion to the argument, but at the same time this comparison does not quite work. However influential and important the function of the high priest may have been, he was and remained a human being – indeed a sinful human being. Therefore the author of the letter to the Hebrews is not content with this comparison between Jesus and the high priest from the Old Testament–Jewish tradition. Jesus was more than one of the series of high priests. Jesus himself was not descended from the tribe of Levi and the family of Zadok from which high priests had to be descended. His origin lay elsewhere. This is the notion which forms the starting point in the letter to the Hebrews for an argument which is as surprising and creative as it is bold and controversial:

Now if perfection had been attainable through the levitical

priesthood (for under it the people received the law), what further need would there have been for another priest to arise after the order of Melchizedek, rather than one named after the order of Aaron (Heb. 7.11)?

The conclusion is harsh but inevitable. The levitical, Old Testament–Jewish priesthood has failed. However, fortunately scripture also knows another priesthood which according to the author of Hebrews is of a higher order. it is said to be embodied in the figure of the mysterious Melchizedek, king and high priest of Salem (Gen. 14.17–20; Ps. 110.4). Therefore Jesus' high priesthood, too, is of another, higher order. He is not high priest after the order of Aaron but after the order of Melchizedek (Heb. 6.20). So he has performed his special service in the sanctuary – without daily repetitions, since he did it once and for all (Heb. 7.27).

## Sacrificer and victim

Gradually in his letter the author of Hebrews keeps extending the metaphor of Jesus as high priest. In the first instance Jesus is compared with the high priest who comes forward as 'mediator' between God and the people on the Day of Atonement. In this way he plays his part in the reconciliation which is brought about by God (Heb. 2.18). That is the beginning, but things cannot stop there. Jesus' high priesthood is of a higher order, because the reconciliation which he mediates has a unique character: it happens once and for all. Now the last step needs to be taken. In the Old Testament–Jewish sacrificial cult a sacrificial animal plays an important role in making atonement. It is not offered to God to assuage God's wrath over the sins of the people. That is certainly what is often thought, but it is more a pagan than a biblical notion. God does not want to see blood, but blood necessarily flows during sacrifices. In the cultic legislation of the Old Testament the sacrifice and the sacrificial animal symbolize the fact that God and human beings are coming into contact with one another again, that they are being reconciled with one another. This is not a one-way traffic – in the sense that the human being hopes in this way to change God's mind – but two-way traffic: through sacrifice and altar human beings turn to God, and through the same altar and sacrifice God turns towards human beings. With this symbolism, which we modern men and women find difficult to interpret, we need to be aware that the temple as a whole and the altar in particular were seen as the place where God's presence has become manifest. God is in heaven and human beings are on earth (Ps. 115.16). There is a distance between them, and that is good, but there is also nearness, and that becomes 'visible' in the temple. That is why so much attention is also paid in the ritual of the Day of Atonement to 'atoning for the sanctuary' (Lev. 16).

It is time to take the last step. Not only has the levitical priesthood fallen short, but the same is also true of the cult as such. The rituals need to be repeated every day – in the case of the Day of Atonement every year. That is necessary, writes the author of Hebrews, and he makes what in the light of the Old Testament–Jewish tradition is a daring statement: 'for it is impossible that the blood of bulls and goats should take away sin' (Heb. 10.4). That simply means that another victim must be sought, which gives rise to the notion that Jesus is not only the high priest who sacrifices but also the victim which is sacrificed: 'when he offered up himself' (Heb. 7.27).

We need not be surprised that when reading the letter to the Hebrews we repeatedly come upon the word 'blood'. It occurs more often than in other New Testament writings. It is not strange, since it is closely connected with the metaphor which the author uses. Here the letter is a great exception within the New Testament. Therefore in applying the theological view of Hebrews we must also note this special place, and again be cautious about directly combining the cultic notions with metaphors used by Paul, which often derived from a quite different cultural and social background.

# 9

# The Blood of Martyrs

## Persecutions

We are gradually coming to the end of the New Testament. There are four writings that we have not yet discussed: the two letters of Peter, the letter of Jude and the last book of the Bible, the Apocalypse of John or Book of Revelation. We have already noted that scholars are seldom agreed on questions of authorship and dating, and this is also the case with the books I have just mentioned. But there can be said to be a degree of consensus. A majority of exegetes think that the two letters of Peter and the Apocalypse of John are rightly put at the end of the New Testament in terms of the date of their composition. The letter of Jude is a case apart: in the context of this investigation into christological reflection in the first century the writing is of little value and therefore I shall not be discussing it further.

In the letters of Peter and the Apocalypse of John we hear the voices of Christians living in the last decades of the first century. A good deal has happened and much has changed. After the middle of the 30s of the first century, first Jews and soon also Gentiles became followers of Jesus Christ. They discovered one another and formed a community. In this way the church set out on its way through history. At the end of the first century, in some places – Antioch is the prime example – Christians could already celebrate fifty or sixty years of their community's existence. After the death of the founders a new generation had taken over.

Time went on and the world kept changing. The years in

which Jesus travelled around Galilee and died in Jerusalem disappeared further and further into the darkness of history. Who could still draw on their own experiences and recollections? Unavoidably the picture of the 'historical' Jesus began to fade. That was not such a bad thing as it might perhaps seem, since in this way space was made in which new images could be created. And that is necessary, since theological insights constantly need to be adapted to changing circumstances. Theology is done within a particular context. There are no objective truths, nor have there ever been. It is regrettable that people still think that there are. The theological insights of evangelists and apostles, the theologians from the first generation of Christians, must be understood and interpreted against the background of time in which they lived and the situation of the community in which they wrote.

It has become clear from our discussion of the theological ideas of the author of the letter to the Hebrews that in the last quarter of the first century the Christian community found itself increasingly confronted with opposition and hostility. Finally, in the middle of the 90s, the first persecutions of Christians took place in large parts of the Roman empire. In the years preceding this outburst of terror and violence, theological reflection slowly began to shift its emphases. As we saw, the letter to the Hebrews can be seen as a telling example of this development.

## The letters of Peter

The beginnings of the two letters suggests that they were written by no less than Peter, one of the key disciples of Jesus and an influential apostle in the early Christian community. However, it has become clear from previous chapters that exegetes are regularly perplexed by introductory questions of this kind. That is also the case here. There is no firm proof and almost everything is open to argument. Why could not Peter have written both letters – or at least the first letter? Those who are inclined to answer this question in the affirmative will increasingly be seized with doubts as they read the letter. Christian legend relates that Peter died as a martyr in Rome in 64 BC in the reign of the emperor Nero. So the letter must have been written before this time. But does it breathe the atmosphere of the period?

That is not completely impossible, but it does seem unlikely. The letter was written in a period of early church history when it was evidently becoming increasingly difficult to be a disciple of Jesus Christ without opposition and hostility. Was the Christian community of Rome in such a position in the time of the emperor Nero? The fire which reduced parts of Rome to ashes led to a short and fierce persecution of Christians which in all probability was limited to the centre of the Roman empire. As I have remarked, persecutions of a less incidental kind which extended over large parts of the territories governed by Rome only arose towards the end of the first century: around two decades after the destruction of the temple in Jerusalem.

If we are to arrive at an adequate assessment of the date of composition of the letters of Peter, further points need to be added to what has already been said. On close inspection both writings raise doubts as to whether they really are letters. They suggest both the letter to the Hebrews and I John. It is also difficult to understand these works as letters in the strict sense of the word. The author of I Peter seems to want to put his readers on the wrong track. He begins with a traditional opening which mentions both the author and those to whom he is writing, and the closing chapter consists mainly of admonitions and greetings, as was usual (I Peter 5.1–14). The same is more or less true of II Peter. But the middle part of the two letters is rather different in character. It lacks the concreteness of Paul's letters. What is written is couched in general terms and gives the impression of not being addressed to one particular group of Christians; rather, it functions as a circular letter intended for a large number of communities. A theological treatise or 'sermon' is being sent as a letter. That also applies to Hebrews and I John, so once again we may assume that the letters of Peter were written in a later stage of early church history: at the end of the first century.

The central theme of I Peter – this letter is more important for our topic than II Peter – is the suffering of the Christian community. Persecutions threaten (I Peter 4.12–16). Martyrdom is slowly but surely beginning to become reality for the followers of Jesus Christ. The perspective on the future is dark and there is sufficient reason for anxiety. However, the author of I Peter does not want to interpret the situation like that. He speaks of joy and gladness. It is worth listening to him for a moment:

> Beloved, do not be surprised at the fiery ordeal which comes upon you to prove you, as though something strange were happening to you. But rejoice in so far as you share Christ's sufferings, that you may also rejoice and be glad when his glory is revealed. If you are reproached for the name of Christ, you are blessed, because the spirit of glory and of God rests upon you. But let none of you suffer as a murderer, or a thief, or a wrong doer, or a mischief-maker; yet if one suffers as a Christian, let him not be ashamed, but under that name let him glorify God.

Human beings suffer, but there are different kinds of suffering. Anyone who suffers as a Christian need not be ashamed of the fact. That is even a reason for joy, because this is a way of taking part in the suffering of Christ. Paul was not afraid of suffering, but the way in which I Peter speaks of the suffering of Christians goes further than the view of the apostle to the Gentiles.

It is evident from the beginning of I Peter how distinctive is the author's view of the place of Christians on this earth. He addresses 'the exiles of the dispersion'. Here in Greek we have a term, *diaspora*, which became very significant in Jewish tradition. *Diaspora* sums up the history of the suffering of the Jewish people down the ages: *diaspora* and exile as a punishment for sins and unfaithfulness, but also *diaspora* as the possibility of fulfilling the age-old promise to Abraham (Gen. 12. 1–3) and being a blessing to all peoples.

Whether on the basis of the term 'dispersion' it could be concluded that the letter is addressed to a Jewish Christian community in the Diaspora is difficult to say with certainty, but the notion cannot be challenged convincingly. It is certainly clear that the term 'exiles' takes on a deeper theological significance in the framework of the letter. The next chapter speaks of 'aliens and exiles' (I Peter 2.11) and here again the terminology makes us think of Hebrews: 'they were strangers and exiles on the earth' (Heb. 11.13), words and concepts which are equally well known to the Old Testament (Ps. 38.13). Those who are chosen by God almost automatically become aliens and exiles on earth. They are no longer 'at home' here. It says a great deal that one of these themes constantly recurs in the summary of witnesses to the faith in Hebrews 11. Here are a couple of typical statements:

> For he looked forward to the city which has foundations, whose builder and maker is God (Heb. 11.10).
> For people who speak thus make it clear that they are seeking a homeland (Heb. 11.14).
> But as it is, they desire a better country, that is a heavenly one (Heb. 11.16).

The author of I Peter would have welcomed such statements sympathetically. Those who follow Christ have become aliens on earth. In that case, slander and blasphemy, enmity and hatred, persecution and martyrdom are no real threat and it can even be said that suffering is an occasion for joy. This is bewildering at first sight, but in the context of the letter it is appropriate and even understandable.

The suffering of the community connects the author directly with the suffering of Christ. That is evident, for example, from the following text:

For it is better to suffer for doing right, if that should be God's will, than for doing wrong.

For Christ also died for sins once for all, the righteous for the righteous, that he might brings us to God, being put to death in the flesh but made alive in the spirit (I Peter 3.17–18).

The christology of I Peter has a traditional character. In scholarly literature it is not unusual for parallels with Paul's letters to be pointed out. However, here it needs to be noted that the atmosphere of I Peter is less disputatious than that of the letters which are attributed to Paul. Nor is discussion of the significance of the Torah a central point of interest (any more). Time has gone on and the context has changed. The suffering of the Christian community as martyrs is beginning to become a reality and the author of I Peter wants to shed light on that. Referring to the suffering of Christ, he hopes that he can encourage the members of his community and give them heart:

You know that you were ransomed from the futile ways inherited from your fathers, not with perishable things such as silver or gold, but with the precious blood of Christ, like that of a lamb without blemish or spot (I Peter 1.18–19).

This attractive text gives a good impression of the way in which christological reflection had developed in the early Christian community in the meantime. Here the author combines a number of well-known metaphors which had already taken on a traditional character: (a) 'ransomed' from the letters of Paul (Gal. 3.13); (b) 'lamb' from the Fourth Gospel (John 1.29, 36); 'blood' from various traditions (Rom. 3.26; Col. 1.20; I John 1.17) and especially from the letter to the Hebrews. It is understandable that in a situation in which the possibility that Christians might die as martyrs for their faith had to be taken seriously, the significance of the blood of Christ increased. Those who were aware that their own blood might possibly soon flow felt all the more akin to the one who had given his blood for the salvation of humankind. At the end of the first century the Christian community began to discover that 'the blood of the martyrs can be the seed of the church'. In this situation the 'theology of the blood of Christ' also began to become more influential. That is understandable in this particular context. However, it does not mean that this metaphor too – and metaphor it is – is valid everywhere and always and should be the only way in which the significance of the suffering and death of Christ can be expressed. Those who do not need to share the fate of the martyrs can hardly adopt their theological views.

Finally, I Peter speaks in traditional terms about the suffering of Christ as 'suffering for others'. However, the author does not stop there. The suffering of Christ is also an example for the members of the Christian community:

> For to this you have been called, because Christ also suffered for you, leaving you an example, that you should follow in his steps (I Peter 2.21).

## The last book of the Bible

In the Apocalypse of John the question is no longer whether the Christian community will be tested by persecutions and martyrdoms. These have already begun and call for victims (Rev. 6.9–10). The author of this work which bears the name of John – it is very improbable that he is identical with the author of the Fourth Gospel – describes himself in the first chapter as 'companion in the tribulation and the kingdom and the patient endurance in Jesus' (Rev. 1.9). We must certainly not envisage his stay on Patmos as an idyll which gives him tranquillity to concentrate on a series of impressive visions. The apocalyptist is on the island of Patmos because he has fled there or has perhaps been deported there.

In terrifying visions he depicts both the present and the near future. The threats to the Christian community are great; evil seems invincible because it has identified itself with the emperor in Rome (Rev. 13). But however bad the situation is and may become, Christians must not lose courage. At the end the light of hope shines out. The believer may know that one day evil will be destroyed – quickly. God's power will overcome the emperor and his ungodly minions. Then a new heaven and a new earth will be created (Rev. 21.1). Then there will be no need for mourning and no one will suffer and die as a martyr, for all enemies and evildoers will disappear for ever from the face of the earth (Rev. 21.8).

What role does Jesus Christ play in this final drama? The question is not easy to answer in a few words. There are even exegetes who do not think it impossible that originally the last book of the Bible was not a Christian work. It bears all too many characteristics of a Jewish apocalyptic expectation of the future for the role and the significance of Jesus Christ to be prominent. Indeed we must take seriously the possibility that an already existing early Jewish apocalypse – comparable to other inter-testamental writings in an apocalyptic spirit, apocalypses attributed to Enoch, Ezra and Baruch – was revised by a Christian author at the time of the first great persecution of Christians at the end of the first century.

The metaphor used in the last book of the Bible for Christ is unique in the New Testament. Moreover that only becomes evident when one is not content with a superficial reading of the text. By far the majority of translations speak of a 'lamb', automatically suggesting that this is related to 'the lamb of God' in the Fourth Gospel (John 1.29,36). However, anyone who takes the trouble of comparing the Greek terms will discover that in the last book of the Bible another term is consistently used. Moreover this term can be translated not only 'lamb' but also 'ram'. What did the writer of the last book of the Bible envisage when he chose this word? In the apocalypse of John, Christ is often compared to a lamb or ram. It is not excessive to suggest that this metaphor is typical of the christology of the last book of the Bible. It is introduced like this:

> And between the throne and the four living creatures and among the elders, I saw a Lamb standing, as though it had been slain, with seven horns and with seven eyes, which are the seven spirits of God sent out into all the earth; and he went and took the scroll from the right hand of him who was seated on the throne.
>
> And when he had taken the scroll, the four living creatures and the twenty-four elders fell down before the Lamb, each holding a harp, and with golden bowls full of incense, which are the prayers of the saints; and they sang a new song, saying,
>
> 'Worthy are you to take the scroll and to open its seals, for you were slain and by your blood you ransomed men for God from every tribe and tongue and people and nation, and have made them a kingdom and priests to our God, and they shall reign on earth' (Rev. 5.6–10).

Here too traditional motifs are unmistakably adopted, worked into a new context and brought up to date. There are references to the suffering of Christ – the lamb is slain – but that does not describe the metaphor completely. The 'lamb that is slain' also functions as a hopeful picture. Precisely this lamb will triumph and at the end of time will sit beside God on the throne (Rev. 22.1–5). The New Testament ends with this grandiose picture. The one who was born in Bethlehem (Matt. 1) sits on God's throne in heaven.

# An 'Exemplary' Life

## No doctrine of the atonement

It is possible that some readers are beginning this last chapter with feelings of confusion and disappointment. At least the classical dogmas and confessional languages spoke a clear language: Christ died on the cross as a complete atonement for all our sins. We have not met this clear language in the writings of the New Testament. The multiplicity of images and metaphors give a chaotic impression: they come tumbling over one another, influence one another and are interwoven with one another; they complement one another, but also contradict one another at the same time. The Bible does not contain a well-rounded and systematic 'doctrine' of the atonement. Evangelists and apostles told stories about the 'historical' Jesus, reacted to questions which were alive in the community and investigated the meaning of the suffering and death of Christ. The New Testament is not only variegated; it also has a fragmentary character. It contains a confusing mixture of visions and views. People are not alike and they do not react in the same way. Whereas one may feel at home in the clear formulations of confessional writings and dogmas, another may have been delighted to recognize the space which the New Testament writings offer.

## Dogmas

However, church history teaches us that the variegated nature of the New Testament was usually seen as a danger rather than as an indication that there should be room within the church and theology for different currents and tendencies. Already at an early stage Christian theologians thought it necessary to sum up the 'teaching' of the church in clear formulas. In the course of the centuries they deliberately developed dogmas and composed confessional writings. In this way they set limits, in the hope of encouraging unity and unanimity with the Christian community. Unfortunately this effort had its tragic side. Anyone who could not subscribe completely to the confessions and doctrinal statements of the church ran the risk of being accused of heresy.

Dogmas have a tendency to multiply. Every dogma produces yet more dogmas. Any formulation of theological viewpoints calls for new clarifications and explanations. Thus gradually a 'doctrine' with a systematic structures comes into being, satisfying the laws of logic and leaving no detail undiscussed. Gradually an impressive dogmatic structure is built upon the theological 'fragments' in the New Testament. Is the New Testament foundation sufficiently firm to support this top-heavy building?

## Believing without dogmas

Anyone who has read the previous chapters will not be surprised to hear that I would answer this last question in the negative. Theologians have thought that they knew more and were even wiser than the New Testament authors. With much creativity and reason they developed a more or less inclusive dogmatic system in which the doctrine of the atonement is central. Jesus' death on the cross was the unique proof not only of God's love for sinners but also of God's punitive justice. God cannot just let evil slip through his fingers. Forgiveness is possible only when the law has run its course. Sin must be punished. It is divine grace that 'in our place' Jesus Christ has borne the punishment and died the death.

Experience teaches us that at present the traditional doctrine of the atonement is an ongoing source of profound conflict. Above all in our modern world the dogma seems to create more problems than it solves. The traditional viewpoints provoke opposition and even irritation. In the debate supporters and opponents often confront each other implacably. Formulations which for one side express the deepest meaning of their faith are brushed aside by the other side as being out of date or even scandalous.

I have not written this book in the hope of putting an end once and for all to such deep-rooted oppositions, which can lead to unpleasant situations in the church and theology. It is impossible to get rid of age-old beliefs in a short time. Moreover it is not my intention to argue that this should be done. The classical dogma also has a right to exist. I do not seek to persuade those who are comforted and encouraged by its formulations to think otherwise. However, I do ask for an understanding of all those who can no longer find themselves in the words of old confessions and dogmas. Honesty compels me to recognize that I myself belong in this category of believers. I know the old and familiar truths of faith, but they no longer move me nor inspire me. The words and images have lost their significance. The excitement has slowly ebbed away.

Questions and problems multiply. The terminology is often felt to be antiquated. But that is by no means the greatest problem. The central content of Christian faith itself is at stake. In the first era of our century Jesus of Nazareth died on the cross in Jerusalem. The church's confession says that his death and atonement brought about reconciliation. But how am I to imagine that? How can the death of someone in a distant past mean salvation and redemption for me, living many centuries later? This notion no longer inspires many people today, but rather provokes opposition. Am I not responsible for the consequences of my own words and actions?

And yet more has to be said. The list of difficulties is not yet exhausted. Even belief in God is involved. In the classical doctrine of the atonement God seems to be his own prisoner. He has to correspond to norms and values which he himself is said to have established. God's mercy is not denied, but his justice is emphasized firmly alongside it. It is this justice which calls for justice to be done, and that can happen only when sin is really punished. For that, blood needs to flow; only that blood can bring about atonement between God and human beings. Is God really in such a strait-jacket? There is the disturbing thought that God is so tied to his own justice that his hands are no longer 'free' to save unconditionally.

The Bible has gradually led me to think otherwise. In the preceding chapters I have tried to demonstrate that no dogmas are formulated in the New Testament writings. Anyone who seeks a clear message will find that a failing. I readily grant that dogma is clearer. The Bible creates more confusion than clarity. Sometimes it seems to be a cacophony of different voices. But I find its variegated nature healthy and a source of inspiration. Many different stories can be told about God. God is good but sometimes also strict; merciful and gracious but sometimes also just. The Bible does not put us in a position to arrive at a balanced judgment. Life is not like that, and the God of Israel is not like that either. He is different from what we think. He is more majestic than we can imagine and loves human beings more than we could believe in our wildest dreams. He does not always correspond to our norms and takes ways which amaze and surprise us. Life with the God of Israel does not go along well-trodden ways, but constantly seems to be an uncertain adventure.

Anyone who wants to discover this surprising and confusing variety in God must first of all read the stories in the Old Testament, and then can also go on to read the New Testament stories about Jesus. He lived close to God in an unexpected and inspiring way. Those who encountered him got as it were a glimpse of God. The early Christian community expressed the divine nearness with the help of various images and metaphors. Jesus is called son of God or image of God. Words are attributed to him which were meant to emphasize the unity between

God and Jesus, between Father and Son: 'He who has seen me has seen the Father.' Evangelists and apostles do not look at the past with the same eyes. Paul directs his gaze consistently to the crucified Jesus and the cross, whereas John puts the incarnation at the centre of his theological reflection. Thus the early Christian community went its way, seeking words and metaphors to express its belief in Jesus Christ. What had he done and what consequences did that have for their life, their thought and their beliefs?

Paul and John, Mark and Matthew, and all those other theologians of the first generation faced a task which was certainly not simple, but can be said to have been extremely exciting. They sensed that the lives had been fundamentally changed. They looked with new eyes on the world around them and at their fellow men and women; they also looked with new eyes at the present and the future; and they dared to suppose that they now also lived in another relationship with God. These changes had not taken place automatically nor did they have themselves to thank for them. Their encounters with Jesus and the stories which had told of him had made them think differently and turned them into different people. Jesus' life and death had an 'exemplary' character. He had made them see that the gulf between heaven and earth, between God and human beings, really could be bridged. Since evangelists and apostles had arrived at that insight, they lived in peace with others and with God. In order to give form and content to these new experiences, hesitantly and cautiously they used words and concepts the scope of which presumably they themselves did not always completely realize: forgiveness of sins, grace, peace, salvation, new creation, justified by faith, freedom, overcoming death, dying and rising to new life, reconciled with God and with their fellow men and women.

We live many centuries later. The 'youthful' experiences of the first generations of Christians do not always speak to us directly. Over the course of the centuries splendid theological systems have been developed, but they no longer satisfy us today. Do we really have to go away with empty hands? Do our words and concepts fall short? That is of course in any case true. I myself see no other possibility than constantly to follow the way back anew and to read the stories in the Bible. In so doing I am fully aware of the distance which separates me from these texts. So today I may no longer be able to affirm them, but I can be guided and inspired by them.

God is in heaven and we human beings live on earth (Ps. 115.16). The distance in itself is not wrong. God gives us freedom to go our own ways on earth. God does not constantly get in our way. Through the Torah his will is not unknown to us and we know the direction which will prove healthy for human beings and the world. However, experience teaches that distance can lead to alienation. The people of Israel also already knew that. Every year on the Day of Atonement the alienation was removed on God's initiative and the possibility of a new start was offered. Jesus is completely in the tradition of scripture. He is the embodiment of God's love and faithfulness. In word and deed he shows who God is. In his life (= incarnation) and death (death on the cross) he bridges the gulf which constantly keeps God and human beings apart. In so doing he also creates a new perspective. His faith in God is 'exemplary' and inspires people, sometimes hesitantly and sometimes enthusiastically, to take the way of reconciliation.

# Index of Biblical References